THE
FROST
&
FESTIVITIES

Discovering Germany's
Uncharted Holiday Wonders

JANINA MOELLER

The Frost & Festivities: Discovering Germany's Uncharted Holiday Wonders

JANINA MOELLER

Published by Pedigree, 2024.

THE FROST & FESTIVITIES: DISCOVERING GERMANY'S UNCHARTED HOLIDAY WONDERS

First edition. October 1, 2024.

Copyright © 2024 JANINA MOELLER.

ISBN: 979-8224087143

Written by JANINA MOELLER.

Table of Contents

INTRODUCTION

You are drawn further into the heart of Germany's undiscovered winter wonders as snow falls over roofs and the aroma of toasted almonds and cinnamon permeates the air. Beyond the glitzy tourist traps, there is a world where tradition quietly thrives, where tranquil towns sprout marketplaces, and where the season's pulse pulses in time with the past. The calm buzz of wooden booths hung with lights and handmade marvels calls with a new type of charm as you explore these snow-covered recesses, unaffected by the sounds of the outside world.

Traveling through the icy regions of Bavaria by rail will drop you off at Mittenwald, a little village tucked away behind the Karwendel mountain range. With its streets lined with pastel-colored cottages that each have murals on their walls conveying a different tale, it seems as if time has stopped here. There is not an overwhelming Christmas market. Rather, it murmurs. Explore the wooden booths with intricately carved nativity scenes made by the local woodcarvers. With warming apple strudel and filling plates of käsespätzle, the gasthaus "Alpenrose" welcomes you in from the cold and chases away the winter blues. The simple and comfortable rooms here provide guests a genuine flavor of Bavarian hospitality without the pomp.

Bamberg, a town farther north, has managed to preserve its medieval heritage, incorporating it into its Christmas market in a manner that evokes a feeling of having fallen through a portal. You may walk past baroque buildings on cobblestone streets to the market, where mulled wine is offered in porcelain cups that make great mementos. As you get closer to Schlenkerla—the town's well-known brewery known for its smoked beer—the aroma of smoked sausages permeates the air.

With a platter of their freshly made bread and regional cheeses, stay warm indoors while the outside cold gradually disappears. Perfectly located in the old town, Hotel Alt-Ringlein provides rooms that combine contemporary comforts with rustic charm, only a short stroll from the market.

❧

BENEATH ITS SNOW-CAPPED summits, Triberg whispers old stories in the Black Forest. The town, which is well-known for its imposing waterfalls, is transformed into a wintry paradise in December. The market is tiny, nestled in amongst the trees, and the cuckoo clocks are silently ticking away in the background, waiting for someone to come admire their classic design. The stands offer hand-carved decorations, wooden toys, and winter specialties like schnapps made in nearby farms and Black Forest ham. The Parkhotel Wehrle in Triberg is the ideal place to unwind after a day of sightseeing thanks to its charming ambience and traditional Bavarian furnishings. The impression that you've discovered something special—something that only a select few will ever encounter—is enhanced by the steam rising from the outdoor hot pools.

With its half-timbered cottages shining warmly in the evening light, Wernigerode awaits you across the country in the Harz Mountains. With merchants selling anything from freshly baked bread to hand-stitched woolen scarves, the market seems cozy. The warmth coming from the vendors selling Feuerzangenbowle, a hot punch mixed with rum, sugar, and mulled wine, outweighs the frost in the air. Get a taste of the renowned Baumkuchen, a tree-ring cake roasted on a spit over an open flame, at Café Wien. Your stay will be further enhanced by the elegant rooms of the neighboring Hotel Fürstenhof, which provide breath-taking views of the Alps.

Traveling east will bring you to Dresden, the home of one of Germany's oldest Christmas marketplaces, the Striezelmarkt. But during the holidays, the city's spirit is found in the smaller, less well-known marketplaces. Nestled along winding lanes, these events include artisanal nutcrackers, Erzgebirge lace, and stollen, a fruitcake that has been sprinkled with powdered sugar since the Middle Ages. Visit the Kastenmeiers restaurant for a lunch that blends contemporary flare with Saxon traditions after perusing the markets.

Long after the final taste, their fresh venison with red cabbage and dumplings is a meal that makes an impression. The Hotel Taschenbergpalais Kempinski in

Dresden provides an opulent way to round off the day, with its historic grandeur serving as the perfect backdrop to the city's festive charm.

⌘

THE LITTLE HAMLET OF Oberammergau, on the outskirts of Munich, is blanketed in snow as its renowned woodcarvers carry on a centuries-old practice of creating elaborate nativity scenes and holy symbols. With lights illuminating the path through the snow-covered alleys, this winter market seems like it sprang naturally from the village's foundations. A cup of hot chocolate from a neighboring vendor warms your hands while you browse, and the experience includes handmade woolen clothes, locally produced honey, and ceramics. With hand-carved hardwood beds and balconies that gaze out over the Alps, the family-run Hotel Alte Post provides accommodations that capture the essence of the rustic beauty of the community.

⌘

THE BERCHTESGADEN AREA, close to the Austrian border, reveals its splendor like a well-kept secret for those looking for even more seclusion. One of the highest peaks in the nation, Watzmann Mountain, overlooks the market located here. Gathering in wooden booths, locals offer aromatic evergreen wreaths, mountain cheeses, and smoked salmon. The sound of alphorns slowly reverberates around the valley in the backdrop, contributing to the otherworldly ambiance. Enjoy hearty quantities of traditional Bavarian dishes like schweinsbraten and knödel at Gasthof Neuhaus, and wash it down with a pint of locally produced beer that is made just next door. Situated high above the town, the Kempinski Hotel Berchtesgaden provides a luxurious and serene alpine experience, complete with floor to ceiling windows that give the impression that you are sleeping in the sky.

⌘

THE TRIP CONTINUES through communities where every chilly blow of wind carries a hint of Christmas cheer. Every town and market has something special to offer, a window into the more subdued and genuine aspects of the season. Markets in Cochem include Riesling wine from nearby vineyards, and the castle overlooking the Moselle River is lit up in a festive magnificence. For those looking for a substantial lunch, a trip to the Zum Kapellen-Driesch restaurant is a must. It is well-known for its slow-roasted meats and locally produced products. With rooms that provide panoramic views of the river and its meandering waters reflecting the dazzling lights from the town below, the Hotel Villa Vinum provides a contemporary stay.

Lübeck is known for its marzipan scent, which permeates the town's chilly air. This market meanders through little lanes, where vendors sell baked products and sweets that are unique to the area. This is the home of Niederegger, the world-famous marzipan maker, where guests may sample the dessert in all of its forms, from simple bars to finely carved figures. Perched on the brink of the Trave River, the historic Radisson Blu Senator Hotel provides the ideal balance of contemporary luxury and easy access to the town's festive celebrations.

THESE MARKETPLACES and these locations seem like discoveries, far from the well-traveled routes used by the average vacationer. As you go from stall to stall, the crunch of snow under your boots catches your breath in the chilly air, and the warmth of the season fills the spaces around you. Every location offers something fresh to discover—a new custom, flavor, or memory just ready to be created. And at the end of the day, you're seated by a fire in a little rural inn, with the faint buzz of the market still resonating in your head.

CHAPTER 1
HIDDEN WINTER MARKETS

IT SEEMS AS IF ONE is entering a long-forgotten winter fantasy when one meanders through the winding lanes of historic German villages. The aroma of mulled wine and roasted chestnuts is a welcome comfort despite the biting cold weather. You discover winter marketplaces that are thriving on long-standing customs in hidden locations that not many outsiders visit. These markets reside in the corners of dense woods and cobblestone villages, kept together by the hands of local artists and decades of craft. They are not the overly publicized, Instagram-glossed events that dominate travel brochures.

For example, Rothenburg ob der Tauber seems to be stuck in the past. The amber glow of Christmas lights softens the stone streets and brings the city's old splendor to life. This market has the atmosphere of a local get-together rather than a tourist attraction. Handmade decorations, candles, and snacks adorn the stalls; many have been handed down through the generations.

Visitors come to love the town's Plönlein, a small, picture-perfect square that seems like it belongs in a fairytale, as they warm themselves with locally made spiced wine and take in the cool night air. Situated in the center of the historic neighborhood, Hotel Herrnschlösschen provides comfortable rooms with a genuine atmosphere. Entering this hotel transports one to a different time period where warmth and history coexist together.

THE BIGGEST ADVENT calendar in the world is created at the town hall of Gengenbach, which is tucked away in the Black Forest. From December 1st to December 24th, a fresh window is opened each evening to display a hand-painted picture that is lit from inside. Familias from all across Germany are drawn to the beautiful sight. Gengenbach is distinctive because of more than just its calendar; its market provides a personal experience where you can watch local artisans create wooden toys or have a cup of Glühwein while sitting by a bonfire and feeling the spirit of the season permeate into your bones. Situated in close proximity to the market, the family-owned Adler Hotel has cozy accommodations that match the warmth of its hospitality. After a day of celebratory roaming, the warm blankets, wooden beams, and views of the forest make it the ideal getaway.

⚜

THE MARKET AT THE HOHENZOLLERN Castle, which is situated on a hill in Baden-Württemberg, is another option. Winding along the little road that leads to the castle with snowflakes swishing in the air and the light of lanterns visible far before the castle itself makes for an almost magical experience. The market takes up the courtyard of the castle, with each vendor tucked behind a historic archway and the scent of roasted nuts blending with the crisp air. Compared to many other markets, it is smaller and less commercial, but that only serves to enhance its allure. Instead than rushing to purchase, visitors stay to experience. The castle provides a striking background for the celebrations, especially while it's snowing outside. The Burg Hotel, which is just a short drive from the castle, has rooms with views of the valley below, making it the ideal spot to take in the scenery while the snow falls.

The half-timbered homes in Quedlinburg, a UNESCO World Heritage site, seem to be bending and leaning against one another due to the weight of generations. They organize a market every December that is nearly mysterious, kept out of sight from big travel groups. Residents' private courtyards are transformed into miniature winter marketplaces for the "Advent in the Courtyards" event. It seems personal to stroll through these areas, which provide a unique glimpse into local life away from the bustle of more marketed celebrations. After a frigid day of exploring, warm lunches of venison and dumplings are served at restaurants like the former royal house Schlosskrug am Dom. Being a guest at Hotel Theophano puts you in the center of Quedlinburg's old town, where you may always be only a short stroll from the seasonal beauty.

Of course, seeing the deep forests of the Black Forest is a must on any tour to Germany's secret winter markets. Tucked among the woods, the market in Triberg, famous for its waterfalls and cuckoo clocks, has wooden kiosks selling everything from schnitzel to schnapps. Even in the dead of winter, the sound of flowing water is constant, and the environment is as unadulterated and unspoiled as it gets.

The Parkhotel Wehrle, a little but quaint lodge, is located close by and provides rustic accommodations with expansive views of the forest, making it the perfect starting point for anybody wishing to explore the market and the surrounding natural beauties.

❧

THE MARKET IN ESSLINGEN am Neckar, close to Stuttgart, is another treasure that transports you even further back in time. With fire-breathers, jousting knights, and artisans pounding away at their forges, it's a medieval-themed market. There's a tangible excitement as the whole town joins in the celebrations. Visitors are given an impression of what Christmas must have been like hundreds of years ago by the absence of contemporary gadgets and the presence of handmade items and lighting. The market in Esslingen is particularly well-known for its performances, which include actors portraying episodes from medieval history and musicians performing on antiquated instruments. The Hotel Am Schillerpark provides comfortable, friendly rooms with period-appropriate décor for guests seeking a truly medieval experience.

The Harz Mountains also possess a certain sort of charm for people looking for marketplaces that are as much about nature as they are about festive happiness. Wernigerode, a village with half-timbered homes that are colorful and snow-covered peaks in the distance, is home to a market where tradition and nature coexist together. While merchants sell traditional foods like smoked sausages and freshly baked bread, local craftspeople sell wood-carved creatures and decorations. Situated in Wernigerode, the Hotel Fürstenhof offers opulent accommodations that combine classic German warmth with convenient market access.

❧

EVEN THE LITTLE BAVARIAN town of Füssen, which is sometimes eclipsed by the neighboring Neuschwanstein Castle, comes to life during its own winter market. A short walk from the market, the Lechfall roars under the freezing water, lending a little of the wild to the joyous occasion. In contrast to the busy tourist destinations nearby, the town itself seems nearly unexplored with its narrow alleyways and old-world charm. Situated close to the market, Hotel Sonne provides cozy accommodations with a contemporary design, making it the ideal spot to unwind after strolling through the snow-covered streets.

Every village and market seems like a window into a bygone winter, maintained not by human effort but by the way these places have always been. They provide more than simply retail; they also provide a feeling of community and a link to the people, place, and customs that define the seasons.

The Charm of Cobblestone Towns

Cobblestone streets meandering through settlements that seem to have not been affected by time, with a light sprinkling of snow. Holiday markets in Germany's lesser-known locations seem like they were lifted straight out of a novel. Imagine the sound of boots against stone and the gentle illumination of lamps from wooden booths. Every turn on the path leads to a secret treasure or another location where time slows down to fit the seasonal rhythms.

Nestled in the Franconia area, Rothenburg ob der Tauber greets you with its ancient walls still standing proudly against the modern landscape. The scent of freshly baked schneeballen, a regional dessert comprised of dough strips formed into balls and coated with powdered sugar, permeates the market square. The villagers assemble, drinking glühwein from tiny porcelain cups while wearing tight-fitting wool jackets and scarves. "Zur Holl" provides a historically inspired dining experience within a short stroll from the busy market. The restaurant's stone walls and flickering candles give it the sense of an old tavern rather than a contemporary one. Even on the coldest winter nights, their roast pork with potato dumplings will keep you toasty, and the aroma of spiced mulled wine permeates the whole space.

THIS AREA'S HOTELS and inns preserve its charm. Consider the 900-year-old "Hotel Reichsküchenmeister," which has quaint accommodations with views of the town's spires and roofs. With its dark wooden beams and ancient furnishings, each room transports visitors to a bygone era, allowing them to experience Rothenburg before the modern world arrived. You may stroll along the slender lanes that are dotted with half-timbered homes from here; each one is more charming than the previous. The town's well-known "Reiterlesmarkt" in December has handcrafted toys, glass decorations, and seasonal sweets that combine the spirit of the season with local customs.

Continue north to Quedlinburg, where tourists may explore one of Germany's oldest and best-preserved cities as cobblestone lanes rise into the sky. Quedlinburg's half-timbered buildings twinkle with gentle lights during the holidays, and evergreen garlands hang from their eaves. Every door you go by appears to be hiding something, and as part of the town's Advent calendar custom, many of them open in December to reveal secret riches. Behind these doors are little, tastefully decorated businesses that provide handcrafted items, traditional candies, and a window into the way of life in the area.

◎⚮◎

THE PANORAMIC VIEW of the town from the "Schlossberg" is something you should definitely see, particularly at night when the streets below are lit up with lights. When it's time for supper, the centuries-old brewery known as "Brauhaus Lüdde" prepares substantial German food. They serve seasonal venison with red cabbage that goes well with a drink of their house-brewed black beer on a chilly winter's night.

The "Romantik Hotel am Brühl" is an accommodation option that perfectly embodies the charm of ancient Quedlinburg. The hotel, which is located in an old house, provides a posh experience without sacrificing the friendliness and warmth for which these communities are renowned. The individually furnished apartments provide a blend of contemporary conveniences and classic style, with a view of the meandering cobblestone streets underneath.

◎⚮◎

BACK TO THE SOUTH, Füssen is tucked away in the Alps, close to the Austrian border. This town is worth visiting for many reasons than simply its close vicinity to Neuschwanstein Castle. Füssen itself has a certain charm, particularly around the holidays when music fills the streets and the aroma of roasted chestnuts permeates the air. Here, the cobblestones appear to lead you through centuries of history, past vividly colored structures that contrast sharply with the snow-covered mountains in the distance. A little but lively Christmas market takes over the town center, offering a selection of regional cheeses, cured meats, and freshly baked lebkuchen. A trip to Füssen wouldn't be complete without dining at the "Ritterstuben," a restaurant built in a structure dating back centuries that was once home to knights. There are wooden beams across the ceiling and a roaring fire to contribute to the cozy, welcoming feeling. Try their handmade spaetzle with cheese and crunchy onions—it tastes even better with a bottle of Riesling from the area.

"Hotel Sonne" provides accommodations for visitors who would want to spend the night, offering contemporary amenities in rooms that preserve the spirit of the town's past. The hotel's decor combines modern flare with classic Bavarian elements, and the balcony views are just amazing. From here, exploring the old town is simple. Cobblestones lead you past frescoes that date back centuries and grace the walls of notable structures.

The intricate network of bridges and winding lanes that span the Regnitz River in Bamberg, located to the east, add to the city's allure. Bamberg, which is well-known for its smoked beer, celebrates the holidays with a market that meanders through the old town, with each vendor selling a distinctive item. Each and every area of the market exudes authenticity, from locally made gingerbread to handmade ceramics. The town's streets seem quite similar to the past as you stroll about them since centuries of footfall have worn the cobblestones smooth.

☙

WITHOUT A STOP TO "Schlenkerla," the recognizable pub where the renowned smoked beer has been made since the 1400s, a trip to Bamberg would not be complete. Warm and comforting delicacies like roasted pig knuckle with sauerkraut are served here, and the scent of the thick, smokey beer fills the air on a chilly winter's evening. When it's time to unwind, the "Hotel Brudermühle," which is close to the river, has accommodations that combine contemporary conveniences with historical beauty. Particularly when covered in snow, the town's vista from the hotel's windows resembles a scene from a fairy tale.

☙

FROM TOWN TO TOWN, the cobblestones continue, each with a unique charm that contributes to the peculiar atmosphere these locations have during the holidays. There's something about these towns that stays long after you leave, whether you find yourself exploring the medieval charm of Monschau, where the smell of freshly made waffles fills the air, or meandering through the winding streets of Görlitz, where the pastel-colored buildings glow under the soft light of streetlamps.

⚜

THE HALF-TIMBERED HOMES of Monschau lean against one another, almost whispering secrets from ages gone by. Situated under the impressive remains of a medieval castle, the tiny and cozy Christmas market offers a wide range of products from locally made beers to hand-knitted scarves. With accommodations that overlook the town's meandering river and winding streets, "Hotel Horchem" offers a warm haven from the winter weather. "Zum Stern" serves classic foods like bratwurst and sauerkraut in a dining room that seems like it hasn't changed in years, making dinner the perfect way to end the evening.

In a way that bigger cities are unable to, these cobblestone villages with their charming marketplaces, old buildings, and winding alleyways perfectly encapsulate the spirit of the Christmas season. They provide a window into a more innocent era when customs are upheld and the allure of the season permeates every wintry breath and sparkling light.

Forest Markets Under the Stars

The fragrance of mulled wine and pine needles permeates the chilly air as lights glimmer in between towering trees. Germany's woodland markets, located far from the congested city squares, provide a new type of magic: a setting where the busy world of contemporary life disappears and the stars seem near enough to touch. These markets are nestled in the middle of old forests, where a cluster of booths that glitter in the winter night are naturally shaded by the tall trees.

The market at Wolfach winds through centuries-old woods deep in the Black Forest. This place exudes a tranquility that can only be found in the forest. Wooden kiosks with handcrafted wooden toys, leather products, and complex metalworks by local artists line the walkways. The aroma of freshly made bread and spicy Lebkuchen competes with the scent of bratwurst cooking over an open flame, and the cozy crackling of the fire beckons guests to stop and mingle.

A LITTLE CLEARING A short distance distant leads to a sitting place where you may take in your treasures. Cozy throws of wool blankets are draped over wooden seats, and little flames in metal pits ward off the cold. Even though the market is teeming with activity, everything has a warmth and gentleness about it that comes from sources other than the flames. The massive, old trees seem to be watching over the celebrations. The sky above opens up, and you can see stars peeping through the branches, giving you the impression that you are far apart from the outer world.

Despite its tiny size, Wolfach offers a few hotel alternatives that are ideal for individuals who like to be near the forest. After a night at the market, the "Hotel Kirnbacher Hof," which is situated outside of the town, provides a comfortable haven. Its wood-paneled rooms' warmth and rustic design blend in well with the surrounding natural environment, making it difficult to leave. A sense of the area is provided by dinner in the hotel's restaurant, where menu items like deer stew are matched with regional wines that capture the essence of the Black Forest.

❧✦❧

SLIGHTLY FARTHER NORTH, in a remote area of the Northern Black Forest, the cool air is filled with the aroma of fresh pine thanks to the Christmas market in Bad Rippoldsau-Schapbach. With only a few vendors, the market seems even more personal here, yet each one captures the spirit of the area. Handcrafted wooden sculptures and traditional woolen clothing made from the fleece of surrounding sheep are among the items sold by the local artisans. Every item in these forests has a past that is almost palpable.

You may explore more of the woodland after browsing the market booths by taking a trek on one of the neighboring paths. The trail meanders through the woods before arriving to the "Sankenbach Waterfall," which is illuminated by moonlight and has icicles that grow along the rocky borders. The ice waterfalls seem to mirror the stars above, giving the picture an ethereal splendor.

❧✦❧

A COMBINATION OF ECO-friendly elegance and rustic charm may be found at the adjacent "Naturhotel Holzwurm" for visitors looking for a unique overnight experience. Large windows that overlook the forest allow natural light to flood the hotel, which was constructed using wood from the area. There's nothing better than heading to the sauna after a long day outside, when the warmth appears to go deep into your bones and dispel the coldness that tends to settle after hours spent outside.

The woodland market in Waldkirchen is another undiscovered treasure when you go east into the Bavarian woodland. This market, which is situated within a natural park, makes the most of its surroundings with its booths braided into the forest and its walkways lit by delicate lights that dangle from the trees. Handcrafted wooden nutcrackers, intricate lacework, and hand-painted glass decorations are among the typical Bavarian goods offered by the sellers here. As guests stroll through the woods, dishes of roasted chestnuts, sausages, and spiced fruit pastries entice them. The cuisine is representative of the regional cuisine.

AFTER CONSUMING EVERYTHING that the woodland has to offer, enjoy a sleigh ride over the neighboring meadows coated in snow. The only sound that disrupts the stillness of the surrounding woods is the crunch of hooves in the snow. The journey seems like traveling back in time to a place where nature is dominant and technology seems far away, especially when you're wrapped up in a thick woolen blanket and the cold air is cutting at your cheeks.

Several tiny guesthouses that suit the spirit of the market are available in Waldkirchen itself. The Bavarian-inspired rooms of "Hotel Gottinger" include carved wood furniture and soft comforters that beckon you to spend the night. Its restaurant is the ideal place to dine after a chilly day of hiking since it provides substantial regional fare like roasted meats and knödel (dumplings).

ONE OF THE MOST REMARKABLE forest markets may be found in the heart of Germany in the Harz Mountains, deep among the mysterious woodlands of the area where the towering pines' shadows linger late into the night. The market is held in the town of Goslar, which is tucked away in a natural clearing that is lit up with glittering lights and gentle lanterns. It seems like entering a hidden realm where the contemporary world disappears and time stops still as you stroll through the market.

Handcrafted wooden figurines, candles, and classic Harz delicacies like Baumkuchen—layered cake grilled over an open flame—are available for purchase from the neighborhood sellers. Observe as every layer of batter is brushed over the cake, creating a beautiful, golden ring that becomes even more delicious when consumed while the fire is burning. With their branches flowing softly in the wind and creating changing shadows over the snow-covered ground, the trees surrounding the market provide a certain something magical to the picture.

After spending the night meandering in the woods, "Hotel Niedersächsischer Hof," which is only a short distance away, provides the ideal spot to relax. Situated on the town's edge, the hotel offers rooms with warm oak furnishings, comfortable beds, and views of the surrounding mountains, all while maintaining a reference to classic German style. This restaurant serves regional wines with dishes like wild animal stew and mushroom stew.

THE HIGHEST MOUNTAIN in the Harz Mountains, the "Brocken," is reached via a route that continues further into the forest. The stillness that only a forest at night can provide permeates the air on a clear night, when the stars seem near enough to touch. Even if the cold scratches at your skin, the scene's splendor makes every second of it worthwhile.

EVERY FOREST MARKET is like entering a another planet, one where the bustle and commotion of daily life seem to disappear and where the trees and stars have created a whole new universe. These marketplaces, where the romance of the holidays seems to linger in every shadow, every gust of wind, and every flashing star above, are defined by the lights hung between the branches, the fragrance of pine and fire, and the taste of spiced wine and roasted chestnuts.

CHAPTER 2
FESTIVE TRADITIONS BEYOND THE MAINSTREAM

GERMANY IS KNOWN FOR more than only its famous Christmas markets and city events. Once you go off the main track, you'll discover a tapestry of local traditions that have been handed down through the years that authentically captures the essence of the season in a manner that can only be experienced personally. There is something special waiting around every corner, from the untamed hills of Bavaria to the meandering valleys of the Rhine, and it is celebrated with coziness, cuisine, music, and long-standing customs. Unaffected by the bustle of the city, these festivities provide something unique and classic.

THE KRAMPUSLAUF, OR Krampus Run, transforms the chilly winter streets of Berchtesgaden, a Bavarian hamlet, into an exhilarating display of both celebration and terror. Men costumed as Krampus, the mythological character that punishes naughty children, run through the town while toting bundles of sticks and rattling chains. They are clothed in intricate, hand-carved masks with diabolical horns. It's a crazy, disorderly event when celebration and tradition come together in a striking show. The Berchtesgaden area offers the ideal backdrop for this age-old custom with its quiet alpine beauty and mountain views. In welcoming pubs like Gasthaus Bier Adam, residents and tourists congregate after the race to enjoy hearty Bavarian delicacies like sauerbraten, käsespätzle, and the ubiquitous glass of Weissbier. A beautiful but authentically alpine refuge, the Hotel EDELWEISS provides a place to relax after the excitement of the evening and panoramic views of the surrounding mountains.

⦿≫≪⦿

HEADING INTO THE BLACK Forest to the west, the community of Gengenbach presents a more subdued, but no less captivating, perspective on holiday customs. Known for its ancient alleyways and half-timbered homes, this little town transforms into a live advent calendar during the holidays. With 24 windows, the town hall becomes a massive advent calendar where a new window is opened every evening to display a work of art or a festive scenario. The whole hamlet comes together to celebrate as local choirs sing carols. The Gengenbach Advent Calendar offers a peaceful but engrossing experience that instills a feeling of childish delight throughout the holiday season. Hotel Die Reichsstadt is a boutique hotel that welcomes guests and offers a warm, personal ambiance. You'll be just a short stroll from the events because to its prime position in the center of the ancient town. After an evening of exploring, guests may warm themselves with regional favorites such Black Forest ham and Maultaschen, a sort of stuffed pasta, at the hotel's restaurant.

⦿≫≪⦿

MONSCHAU, A TOWN THAT seems to have been stuck in time, may be found in the Eifel area to the north. Its centuries-old homes and winding cobblestone walkways dangle over the freezing Rur River, and come wintertime, it becomes a winter paradise. With kiosks selling handmade items like wooden toys and woolen scarves, as well as sparkling lights reflecting off the river, Monschau's Christmas market evokes the feeling of being within a snow globe. Monschau is not simply known for its market, however; its annual Christmas torchlight parade is a sight to see. The old stone walls are illuminated by the torches carried by locals wearing medieval costumes as they make their way through the narrow alleyways, giving the holiday season an air of historical significance. If you choose to spend the night, the 18th-century *Hotel Horchem*, which is situated right on the riverfront, has character-filled rooms that blend old-world beauty with contemporary conveniences. Local dishes are served in the hotel's restaurant, and the riverbank terrace offers an absolutely breathtaking view of the town covered in snow.

⌒⌒⌒

LÜBECK, IN NORTHERN Germany, is well-known for its marzipan during the holiday season. However, the little town of Ahrensbök, not far from the city, has a lesser-known custom called Lübsche Wiehnacht. This joyous occasion, which takes place in a nearby manor home, honors Lübeck's historical traditions by presenting period-appropriate Christmas festivities. The manor's great halls are decked up in period detail, and players dressed in period attire present plays, narrate Christmas stories, and sing traditional German songs. Visitors may explore the grounds with a cup of spiced cider in hand, bake traditional Christmas sweets, or take part in candle-making activities. It's a once-in-a-lifetime opportunity to witness Christmas as it was celebrated in northern Germany centuries ago. After a day at the manor, *Schlossgut Gross Schwansee*, a classy 18th-century estate turned hotel, is not far away and provides opulent lodging in a picturesque location. Its restaurant offers upscale regional cuisine with an emphasis on organic, locally sourced products, making your visit as enjoyable as it is joyous.

⌒⌒⌒

SEIFFEN, A TOWN STEEPED in centuries of mining history, is a destination for anyone prepared to trek into the isolated towns of the Ore Mountains (Erzgebirge). Here, Christmas customs are still firmly established in the past. Seiffen, often called the "toy village," is well-known for its nutcrackers, Christmas pyramids, and hand-carved wooden figurines, all of which are created by regional artisans who have been passing down their knowledge for many years. The town's yearly Mettenschicht (Miners' Christmas) festival, which honors the area's mining background, is a poignant event. Locals in traditional mining attire go to the church by candlelight, singing songs that reverberate off the snow-covered mountains. Following the ritual, a bustling marketplace comes to life where you may buy locally made decorations, savor freshly made Stollen, or sip Glühwein by the fireplace. After a hard day, the *Hotel Seiffener Hof* provides a warm, rustic retreat with classic wooden furniture and a restaurant offering substantial Saxon fare like sauerbraten and Kartoffelsuppe.

⁊⨳⨳

THE FEUERZANGENBOWLE festival is a distinctive celebration held by the little town of Trippstadt in the middle of the Palatinate Forest. This flamboyant event centers on a strong mulled wine punch, ignited by a rum-soaked sugar cake. The gathering, which takes place in the town square, gathers residents and guests around crackling bonfires to share tales, laughs, and mugs of the fiery beverage. The snow-covered woodland gives an ethereal atmosphere to the celebrations.

Because the village is close to the forest, guests may enjoy a guided winter trek before coming back for the celebrations. Situated little outside of town, the *Hotel Schlossberg* provides a quaint location to stay with roomy accommodations overlooking the forest. The hotel's restaurant is the ideal way to cap off a day of winter exploration, serving substantial regional cuisine with a concentration on dishes including wild game.

⁊⨳⨳

HIDDEN AWAY IN LITTLE towns and isolated villages, these joyous customs provide a window into Germany that many visitors fail to see. These festivities, which are held away from the flash and materialism of big cities, cling to something more ancient and intimate: a centuries-old bond with the land, the people, and the spirit of the season.

The Mystical Raunächte Nights

S omething old stirs in the German countryside in the dark stillness of winter, when the world is hushed after Christmas and the new year draws near. The twelve mysterious nights known as the Raunächte, which fell between December 25 and January 6, had a supernatural effect on both communities and woodlands, drawing people into a bygone era of magic, superstition, and introspection. This is the moment to discover the unadulterated mystique of winter, tucked between light and dark, tradition and time.

The Raunächte people of Oberammergau, in the Alps, have ancient traditions that are based on both pagan and Christian mythology. Houses are thoroughly cleansed to drive out any ghosts from the previous year, and to ward against misfortune, herbs and frankincense are burnt at entrances. Known for its Passion Play and woodcarvers, Oberammergau becomes something more on certain evenings. Lanterns hanging by the windows cast a gentle flicker, illuminating the town's carved façade. Ghost tales are chilling; they are whispered by the fire. It is not unusual to come across people engaging in centuries-old rituals; their actions are motivated by the conviction that these evenings serve as a portal between the realm of the living and the ghosts of the past. The warm, stylish rooms of the *Hotel Maximilian* in Oberammergau, with their hefty oak furnishings, are the ideal location to recuperate after a night out in the cold. Ammergauer Stub'n, the on-site restaurant, offers substantial Bavarian fare like dumplings and venison stew, which is the ideal comfort meal at this enchanted time of year.

THE RAUNÄCHTE BECOMES much more jagged as you go more north to the Harz Mountains. People assemble at Wernigerode, a town perched high on the edge of a forest, for the "Perchtenlauf," a frightening parade of masked characters said to ward off bad spirits. It's easy to feel as if you've slid into one of the Brothers Grimm's darker stories on these evenings since this is the country where many of their fairy tales are located. Carrying burning torches, the villager's shadows dance along the medieval structures as they march through the streets dressed in furs and hideous wooden masks with hideous expressions. Due of their shared interest in the ethereal and mysterious, residents and visitors alike come together for this occasion. Nestled next to Wernigerode Castle, the *Schlosshotel Wernigerode* is the perfect location to stay, offering a blend of contemporary luxury and old-world charm. The hotel's restaurant serves local delicacies like Harzer cheese and wild boar sausages, and its accommodations provide expansive views of the forest and castle.

The Raunächte have a more contemplative, mystical aura in the more sedate areas of Lower Bavaria. Tiny towns scattered over the wintry terrain illuminate their roads with candles, and the inhabitants use these evenings to pay tribute to their forefathers and carry out age-old traditions connected to the crop and the land. During a Raunächte ritual in the hamlet of Bad Griesbach, bonfires are lit in the fields and people walk through the snow to bless the ground and ensure that there would be an abundance of crops the next year. The chilly night air is charged with the prospect of the unknown, with a strong aroma of fire and pine. Locals retire to *Hotel Das Ludwig*, an opulent spa resort encircled by snow-covered woodlands, after the festivities. After spending the night outdoors, guests may unwind in the thermal baths and saunas here, feeling the cold take off of their bones. With a focus on using seasonal, local foods like woodland mushrooms and freshly caught fish from neighboring lakes, the hotel's restaurant serves farm-to-table cuisine.

❦

THE RAUNÄCHTE OVER in the enigmatic Black Forest change the surrounding area into a scene straight out of a folktale. People assemble in the community of Triberg, which is well-known for its beautiful waterfalls and clockmaking customs, to participate in the "Rauhnachtwanderung," a midnight stroll through the forest. They go through the snow-covered woods stealthily, guided only by the light from lanterns. At old trees, they conduct rituals and give presents to the ghosts who are said to roam the area. Mythical creatures are easily imagined to be hiding in the shadows during these evenings in the Black Forest, which has traditionally been shrouded in mystery. With comfy rooms and a hearth, the local guesthouse *Best Western Plus Schwarzwald Residenz* provides a warm haven after a strenuous night of exploring the woods. As morning emerges over the woods, guests may have a typical Black Forest breakfast of dark bread and smoked ham.

The atmosphere around the Raunächte becomes more joyous in the southern parts of Franconia, especially in the vicinity of Rothenburg ob der Tauber. Cobblestone streets meander past half-timbered cottages and historic turrets in this exquisitely maintained medieval village, all softly lit by candlelight. This place celebrates the Raunächte with music, storytelling, and feasts. Four townhouses from the 16th century house the *Hotel Eisenhut*, where visitors are treated to tasteful rooms steeped in history. The restaurant features regional wines from the nearby vineyards along with a blend of Franconian and foreign cuisine. Following supper, guests may embark on a Raunächte-themed night tour with a local guide, during which they will travel through the town's secret passageways and hear tales of ghosts, witches, and evil sorcery.

❦

OBERSTDORF, A HAMLET in the Allgäu area, provides a more nature-focused Raunächte experience among the snow-covered hills. People believe that during these twelve days, the souls of the Alps descend to wander the earth, therefore evenings are spent here in serious contemplation of the mountains. In their mountain huts, the locals get together to share tales, food, and drink, and to pray for the protection of their families and cattle in the next year. Situated on a hillside with sweeping views of the neighboring peaks, the *Alpe Dornach Mountain Lodge* offers a remarkable spot to stay. The rustic rooms have a cozy, welcoming feel to them thanks to their thick wool blankets and wooden beams. Together with regionally made beers, guests may savor traditional Allgäu fare like Schweinshaxe (pork knuckle) and käsespätzle (cheese noodles).

❦

THE RAUNÄCHTE ARE MORE than simply a group of antiquated customs across Germany. They provide a profoundly spiritual link to the land, to the ancestors, and to the winter's secrets. Immersed in myth and enchantment, these twelve nights unveil the secret essence of the season, which stays elusive until you are there to see it for yourself.

Swabian Yuletide Rituals

During the holidays, Swabia, in the center of Baden-Württemberg, comes to life with a rich tapestry of customs that harken back to ages past. These practices turn the long winter evenings into a time of celebration, warmth, and a strong sense of community among the charming towns and rolling hills. Swabian Yuletide customs transport guests to a realm where contemporary celebration blends with legend, producing a mystical experience that is unique to this area.

Towns like Tübingen become hubs of activity as December approaches. The old marketplace is transformed into a paradise of dazzling lights, wooden kiosks, and fragrant delights during the Christmas market. Around to taste bratwurst frying on the grill, residents and tourists alike pour generously of glühwein, a spicy mulled wine. With robust foods like *Maultaschen* (Swabian dumplings) and *Käse Spätzle* (cheese noodles), this market offers the ideal introduction to Swabian tastes. Carolers singing traditional tunes are accompanied by the laughter of families strolling around the market. Excitement permeates the air, as the scents of gingerbread and roasted chestnuts meld. If you want to go even deeper, the adjacent *Hotel Am Schloss* provides a classy lodging with breathtaking views of Tübingen Castle and a restaurant that serves regional food.

AS ONE TRAVELS FURTHER into Swabia, the quaint town of Esslingen, with its lovely medieval core, is home to one of the oldest Christmas markets in the area. With a twist, the market embodies the spirit of a classic Yuletide celebration. Stalls selling handcrafted items and local specialties are available for visitors to peruse, but what really draws them in is the chance to see the *Nikolauslauf*, a distinctive procession that happens in early December. A local performer dressed as Saint Nicholas leads a group of naughty Krampuses—horned characters who symbolize the bad side of the holiday—as they march through the streets. Crowds are drawn to this energetic show, which combines amazement and hilarity. After that, relax at *Weinstube am Stadtgraben*, a little wine bar tucked away that's well-known for its wide array of regional wines and welcoming ambiance.

If you go farther into the Swabian countryside, you'll discover the charming Yuletide traditions of the little community of Bad Urach. The *Adventmarkt*, which takes place during the four weeks preceding up to Christmas, is celebrated by the inhabitants here. Local artists offer their created items there, ranging from elaborate wooden toys to candles produced by hand. The town square is illuminated with lanterns and candles as the sun sets, creating a cozy ambiance that beckons people to congregate and exchange tales. Gathering for customary holiday pursuits like cookie crafting and tree decoration brings families closer. After perusing the market, visitors may unwind in comfort at the *Hotel Graf Eberhard*, which is tucked away on the outskirts of the charming village. The hotel provides contemporary amenities together with classic Swabian hospitality. One of the hotel's dining options is its seasonal restaurant, which guarantees a delightful dining experience.

FOR THOSE WHO ARE INTERESTED in the esoteric aspects of the holidays, Weingarten offers an enthralling custom called the *Bergaufzug*. Every December, locals make a trek up the nearby hill, singing and carrying candles along the way. This festive but somber occasion celebrates the approach of winter and the expectation of a prosperous new year. The ambience is peaceful and quiet, providing a moment of reflection in the middle of the busy season. When partygoers go back to the town, they may visit the neighborhood *Gasthaus zur Traube*, where the smell of handmade stew and the cozy fireplace will greet them. This hotel, which is well-known for its substantial regional cuisine, epitomizes Swabian friendliness.

The sleepy town of Biberach becomes a sight out of a fairytale as Christmas draws near. The *Krippenspiel*, a live nativity play that embodies the spirit of the holidays, draws people from the local community. Everyone is engaged in a participatory experience as both adults and children dress as characters from the Nativity tale. The show takes place in the town center, which is flanked by tastefully adorned chalets serving traditional fare like spiced apple cider and *Lebkuchen*, or gingerbread. Following the performance, guests may unwind at the *Hotel Biberacher Hof*, a quaint venue with rustic furnishings and a dedication to using local products in their cuisine, letting patrons enjoy the tastes of the area in a cozy, friendly setting.

Starting on the evening of Epiphany, the custom of *Fasnet* is another fascinating facet of Swabian Yuletide festivities. Locals dress up in masks and costumes for this carnival-style festival, which lasts for many weeks. Drums beating and bands playing upbeat music, the colorful procession in cities like Rottweil lights up the streets. Playful pranks are exchanged, honoring traditional traditions while capturing the spirit of the season. The event enthralls people of all ages and fosters a joyous, laugh-filled environment. *Hotel Rottweil* is a boutique hotel that offers accommodations that combine contemporary conveniences with historic charm. It's the ideal starting point for exploring the town's exciting festivities.

The Yuletide season, which weaves together customs that transcend centuries, reflects a feeling of solidarity and goodwill in the heart of Swabia. This area offers discovery and celebration around every turn, from vibrant marketplaces to peaceful rural customs. Swabia provides a charming window into the center of holiday celebrations as you stroll through light-filled cobblestone streets, enjoy the comforts of regional food, and take part in the lively customs that envelop you in happiness.

CHAPTER 3

SNOW-COVERED CASTLES AND PALACES

GERMANY IS TRANSFORMED into a place straight out of a fairy tale as the winter winds blow over the country, setting snow-covered castles and palaces against a beautiful, crisp sky. Explore these historical masterpieces, each enhanced by a snowy coating that adds to their beauty and attraction, during this lovely season.

Start your adventure in the most well-known castle of them all, Neuschwanstein Castle. Tucked up in the heart of the Bavarian Alps, this magnificent building seems to have been lifted right out of a novel. Under a new covering of snow, the castle looks especially enchanting with its majestic turrets and tall spires. This famous location sees fewer visitors in the winter, making for a more personal encounter. Discover the magnificent rooms of the castle, notably the Music Hall, which has stunning paintings and an enthralling chandelier that shimmers like icicles. Cozy accommodations like the *Hotel Müller Hohenschwangau*, which is close by and gives breathtaking views of the castle, are available in the quaint town of Hohenschwangau. Savor a substantial Bavarian lunch at *Alpenstuben*, a neighborhood eatery well-known for its mouthwatering schnitzel and apple strudel, after a day of sightseeing.

THE NARRATIVE THEN moves north to the imposing Heidelberg Castle, which is positioned atop the Königstuhl hill and provides a stunning view of the city. This castle stands out against the wintry background because to its exquisite fusion of Renaissance and Gothic architecture. The expansive gardens and historic walls of the castle grounds provide for enjoyable strolls and plenty of picture opportunities. The adjacent Old Town comes alive in the evenings, particularly when the plaza hosts the Christmas market. Handmade products abound from vendors, and the air is filled with the fragrance of roasting almonds. *Kulturlokal* is a hidden treasure in the area that serves delicious seasonal meals made with fresh ingredients from neighboring farms.

⸻❧⸻

EXPLORE THE FANCIFUL appeal of the Meissen Albrechtsburg Castle, which is located further east and is regarded as Germany's first castle constructed primarily for domestic use. Under a covering of ice, its Gothic architecture glistens, offering a distinctive setting for winter exploration. Meissen is known for its porcelain, therefore stories of monarchs and artists may be found in the castle's colorful past. Don't pass up the chance to see artisans at work crafting beautiful pieces at the neighboring Meissen Porcelain Manufactory. In the center of Meissen, the *Hotel Goldener Löwe* provides cozy accommodations and a delicious breakfast that includes regional delicacies, making it a great choice for a memorable visit.

The castle of Schwerin calls with its picturesque lakeside location as you continue your journey. The snow-dusted towers are reflected in the shimmering waterways around the castle, producing an amazing winter scene. This architectural marvel displays a complex tapestry of history by fusing features of many styles, from Renaissance to Gothic. While the snow-covered royal grounds still beckon investigation, the huge ballroom within mesmerizes with its splendor. After a day of seeing castles, enjoy a comfortable night's sleep at the *Hotel Niederländischer Hof* in the neighboring city of Schwerin. Fresh fish and seasonal cuisine at the neighborhood eatery *Peters eatery* provide a sense of the area.

⸻❧⸻

TRAVELING TO MUNICH, you will find the magnificent Nymphenburg Palace, which is located in the center of Bavaria. Set inside a wide park, this enormous Baroque mansion is ideal for winter stroll amid the white-draped trees. The exquisite halls of the palace, such as the magnificent Gallery of Beauties, enthrall guests with their grace. With its collection of priceless artwork and historical relics, the palace museum provides an insight into the lifestyle of the Bavarian nobility. After touring, treat yourself to dinner at *SchwabenQuellen*, a distinctive eatery with traditional Bavarian cuisine and a warm, inviting ambiance that's perfect for a wintry winter's day.

The charming village of Landsberg am Lech, not far from Munich, is home to the majestic Landsberg Castle. Discovering this lesser-known treasure gives tourists an opportunity to have a more intimate look at Bavarian history. The castle offers an evocative environment for exploration with its spectacular views of the Lech River and medieval architecture. During the holidays, the quaint town square is decked up with lights and decorations, inviting guests to enjoy the local restaurants. Try *Gasthaus Zur Post* for a fascinating culinary experience, where meals cooked from scratch capture the essence of the area.

❦

HEADING EAST, THE ENTHRALLING fortress of Burg Kreuzenstein, close to Vienna, lies in wait. This 19th-century castle offers guests a one-of-a-kind experience by combining contemporary conveniences with features of medieval grandeur. While relics gathered from many locations narrate tales of knights and wars, the surrounding surroundings entice investigation. After your journey, be sure to stop at the *Burg Kreuzenstein Restaurant* in the adjacent village of Leobendorf, which serves delicious meals while offering a view of the castle.

The beautiful architecture and the joyous atmosphere that permeate the air are only two of Germany's wintertime charms. With its own history and personality, every castle and palace becomes a fantasy that entices guests to enjoy the holidays in a really enchanted manner. Whether seeing opulent buildings, savoring regional cuisine, or just taking in the tranquil beauty of wintry scenery, these ancient locations evoke enduring memories. Every visit is a treat for the senses—a window into history, a link to customs, and a heartwarming and imaginative celebration of the season.

Neuschwanstein's Winter Fairytale

The castle known as Neuschwanstein stands as a symbol of winter enchantment in the center of Bavaria, where the mountains reach the sky. The castle, with its turrets and spires right out of a fairy tale, seems like a scene out of a novel as snowflakes dance through the air. Travelers from all over the globe are drawn to this famous site because of its allure, particularly in the winter when its ethereal beauty is even more striking.

The trip starts in the quaint town of Hohenschwangau and ends at the castle. This charming location, tucked away in a valley, has a homey feel to it with its warm lodges and friendly eateries. A great starting point is the *Hotel Müller Hohenschwangau*, which offers cozy accommodations with breathtaking castle views. Once they've settled in, visitors may take a leisurely walk about the hamlet, where holiday lights glimmer against the snow-capped hills. The neighborhood café, *Café Müller*, is well-known for its delicious pastries and handcrafted delicacies. Warm up with a cup of hot chocolate there.

An enchanting experience may be added to the journey to the castle by taking a picturesque stroll or a horse-drawn carriage ride through the wintry scenery. The trail winds through snow-covered trees, the faint sound of hoofbeats resonating in the distance against the quiet. When you arrive at the castle gates, the view is just amazing. With a fluffy blanket of snow above, Neuschwanstein has an almost unearthly aura.

KING LUDWIG II'S OPULENT preferences are evident throughout the castle's chambers; the Throne Room, with its ornate chandeliers and minute detailing, epitomizes royal splendor. Guests may imagine the lavish parties that formerly took up this area while marveling at the beautiful workmanship. Ludwig's favorite place to see brightly painted murals honoring the arts and culture is the Singing Hall. Wintertime exploration of the castle grounds offers special views, as the surrounding area becomes a glistening paradise. Photographers are invited to take mementos of the castle against the background of the Alps at the Marienbrücke, a bridge that offers breathtaking views. It is a moment to treasure to see Neuschwanstein rise magnificently over the icy lake below.

⚜

A DAY OF EXPLORING is over, and Hohenschwangau's warm ambience beckons. Hearty Bavarian food is served in restaurants like *Alpenstuben*, which is ideal for refueling after a cold day. Savor classic delicacies like spätzle and schnitzel while sipping a cool regional beer. A feeling of community is fostered by the welcoming atmosphere, which is filled with laughing and discussion. There are several quaint lodges scattered around the surroundings of Hohenschwangau for those who want to prolong their visit. For those seeking a more refined experience, the *Schloss Hohenschwangau Hotel* has exquisite dining options and lovely accommodations. Enjoy breakfast every morning while taking in expansive views of the neighboring mountains, which sets the mood for an exciting new day of exploration.

⚜

THE REGION IS A PARADISE for outdoor lovers, with plenty of winter sports available. Ice skating and ice fishing are encouraged on the neighboring Forggensee lake, which is often frozen throughout the winter. Hohenschwangau rental businesses provide equipment for anyone who can't wait to feel the winter cold. All ages enjoy the thrilling sensation of gliding over the ice with the castle as a background.

⚜

THE CASTLE BECOMES charming in a new way when night sets. Glistening like a diamond against the pitch-black sky, Neuschwanstein is illuminated. At night, Hohenschwangau presents a distinct image of itself, with residences and businesses adorned with sparkling lights. To add to the Christmas spirit, seasonal markets appear, providing handmade items and festive food.

There are still culinary marvels to entice every taste. Take *Restaurant Neuschwanstein*, which is well situated close to the castle. This restaurant offers a cozy and welcoming ambiance and is well-known for its seasonal cuisine and regional delicacies. Guests may savor cuisine that really captures the characteristics of the area by consuming fresh products from neighboring farms.

Travelers from all over the world are drawn to Neuschwanstein Castle by its charm, hoping to experience its winter enchantment. An amazing experience is produced when magnificent architecture, fascinating history, and spectacular scenery come together. Every minute spent here seems like it might be taken straight out of a fairy tale, whether you're touring the castle's magnificent rooms, enjoying authentic Bavarian food, or basking in the peace of the surrounding woodlands. The event is even more magical for families. Whether they are making snowmen, sliding down slopes, or going on treasure hunts through the snow-covered forests, kids enjoy the wintertime pastimes. Hohenschwangau's welcoming environment encourages relationships as families laugh and tell tales in front of the castle.

THE MORE WINTERTIME we get, the more alluring Neuschwanstein seems. Every winter turns the castle's grounds into a blank slate ready for exploration. The allure of Neuschwanstein during the winter season never goes out of style, fulfilling the hopes and wishes of those who have been through its halls, whether they are returning or coming for the first time.

Visitors may discover a haven from the daily grind in addition to an amazing historical place in this winter paradise. The peacefulness of the snow-covered surroundings and the friendliness of the Bavarian people come together to create a calm haven where every second encourages introspection and fellowship. Neuschwanstein becomes more than simply a place to visit as hearts overflow with happiness and amazement; it becomes a treasured experience, an enduring memory, and a winter fairytale that endures long after the snow melts.

The Palaces of Potsdam in Winter's Embrace

Travelers are drawn to Potsdam, a gem located just outside of Berlin, by its enchanted palaces, especially in the winter when the surrounding area is covered in a layer of frost. The enchantment of the season mixed with the old buildings' appeal creates a royal but cozy ambiance. A beautiful combination of history and winter wonder may be found while wandering around the Dutch Quarter or the gardens of Sanssouci.

Sanssouci Palace, the crown gem, towers magnificently against a background of woods covered in snow. Its tiered gardens and Rococo architecture enchant guests to this old vacation home of Frederick the Great. The opulent interiors of the palace, each room whispering a history, are revealed during a guided tour. The rooms are decorated with great artwork and magnificent chandeliers. Even in the winter, *Sanssouci's Gardens* are open for exploration and provide guided tours for visitors. Photographs of the charming image created by the snow-dusted sculptures flanking the walks are ideal for preserving memories.

THE NEW PALACE, NEARBY, has a distinct charm. The lavishness of the Prussian monarchs is reflected in its opulent grandeur and ornate ornamentation. The opulent décor and marble hallways whisk visitors back in time. The surrounding parkland, with its frozen walks and peaceful lakes, invites nature lovers, even as the castle itself captivates. Winter's delicate beauty is revealed during a walk around the gardens, where the peaceful atmosphere is accentuated by the sound of falling snow.

This wintry paradise offers cozy hideaways. The *Schlosshotel Potsdam* offers opulent lodging by fusing comfort and style. Guests may relax at the hotel's spa, which offers a variety of treatments that take the edge off, after a day of sightseeing. *Die Garküche*, the hotel's restaurant, invites guests to savor a feast that soothes the spirit with seasonal cuisine made with regional ingredients.

❧

THE PALACES CHANGE as dusk draws in with a gentle glow of lights. The aroma of mulled wine and roasted chestnuts permeates the air as winter markets come to life. Locals and visitors alike are drawn to the *Potsdam Christmas Market* in the historic city center, which offers handcrafted goods, homemade decorations, and delectable food. Warm beverages are available while browsing the booths, many of which include distinctive goods and souvenirs that are ideal for taking a little bit of Potsdam home with you.

One of Potsdam's famous gates, the lovely *Nauener Tor*, is just a short stroll from the market. The lit edifice stands boldly as darkness falls over the city, beckoning a closer inspection. The *Brandenburger Straße*, which is dotted with stores and cafés, is bustling with activity nearby. Cozy places like *Café Lichtenberg*, renowned for its delicious pastries and creamy coffee, are great places for guests to warm up. A slice of Black Forest cake is the perfect complement to a hot cup of tea, making it the perfect place to stop for a snack or exploring day.

❧

A GREEN HAVEN FROM the winter cold is the *Orangerie* in Sanssouci Park, for visitors looking for a more sedate experience. Exotic plants that flourish in warm climates are on display in this magnificent greenhouse, making a striking contrast with the chilly surroundings. Wandering among the vivid greenery allows tourists to temporarily forget about the cold outdoors while taking in the vivid colors and aromatic air.

❧

ANOTHER TREASURE IN Potsdam, the *Cecilienhof Palace*, is located nearby and has an interesting history as the location of the 1945 Potsdam Conference. Among the other palatial buildings, the palace's architecture, which combines German and English Tudor styles, is particularly striking. Exhibitions indoors highlight important historical events that occurred here, enticing history buffs to discover more about the past. Even if it's quiet in the winter, the surrounding gardens have a certain allure that makes for a tranquil walk in the embrace of nature.

The charm of winter eating beckons as the day draws to a close. *Restaurant Ristorante Villa Monte* is a welcoming Italian restaurant with a soft lighting setting. Fine wines and seasonal cuisine combine to make for a memorable dining experience. Guests are left feeling content and prepared to welcome the evening after savoring the chef's unique winter risotto.

⸎

THE *KONGRESSHOTEL Potsdam* offers contemporary conveniences in a historically significant environment for lodging that immerses visitors in the past. It's a great starting point for exploration, with cozy accommodations and quick access to nearby sites. A delicious breakfast buffet is served in the hotel's restaurant, providing guests with fuel for a full day of seeing the palaces.

Wintertime in Potsdam is spectacular in every way. The experience lifts the soul, whether strolling through Sanssouci's gardens, seeing the New Palace's opulent rooms, or just lounging in a cozy neighborhood café. The city beckons exploration, offering stunning views and undiscovered treasures around every corner. With its own charm and background, every palace adds a level to the captivating drama that takes place in this enchanted winter wonderland.

⸎

A SENSE OF AMAZEMENT is evoked in tourists as they stroll along the paths covered with snow, feeling the crisp air and the gentle crunch underfoot. Potsdam's stunning architecture and the allure of the wintertime turn the city into a fantasy realm. The castles speak their tales with every visitor, forging a lifelong bond with this extraordinary location. Winter in Potsdam provides an incredible experience that is just waiting to be had, whether it is by strolling through magnificent halls, indulging in delectable cuisine, or just taking in the ambience.

CHAPTER 4
FROSTY FEASTS AND CULINARY WONDERS

THE CULINARY LANDSCAPE in Germany becomes a sensory extravaganza as winter shrouds the country in white, beckoning residents and visitors to savor the bounty of the season. A tapestry of tastes unfolds, honoring time-honored customs and creative takes on traditional meals, from crowded Christmas markets to tiny eateries nestled away in lovely towns.

It is impossible to experience Germany's wintry gastronomy without also taking in the lively ambiance of its Christmas markets. Imagine this: sparkling-light-adorned kiosks filled to the brim with handcrafted trinkets and gourmet delicacies. One of the most well-known marketplaces, the *Nuremberg Christkindlesmarkt*, is where one may experience the enticing scent of spiced mulled wine, or Glühwein, and roasted almonds. Nuremberg sausages, the market's specialty, entice guests with their deep taste and are best consumed warm off the grill with a side of sauerkraut. The market also offers Lebkuchen, a famous gingerbread biscuit that is sometimes adorned with elaborate icing decorations, for those who want a sweeter treat.

DISCOVER ANOTHER GASTRONOMIC treasure while visiting the charming city of *Dresden* during the holiday season: the *Dresden Striezelmarkt*, known for its famous stollen. This fruitcake epitomizes German holiday baking, with its marzipan filling and powdered sugar coating. Visitors and locals alike go to the market to try the freshly made stollen, which is usually served warm with a cup of coffee. The market enhances the happy atmosphere with a beautiful selection of homemade products and holiday decorations.

Cozy eateries hidden away in charming villages provide an intimate atmosphere for enjoying rich winter cuisine, in contrast to the busy marketplaces. In *Bamberg*, the *Gasthaus Brauerei* provides traditional Franconian fare, such as *Schäufele* (pork shoulder) and *Kloß* (potato dumplings), which are served with beers made in the area. Warmth permeates the air, making it the perfect place to unwind after a day of sightseeing. It's advisable to make reservations since this undiscovered treasure attracts both residents and tourists looking to enjoy genuine Bavarian friendliness.

MEANWHILE, A TRIP TO the *Hofbräuhaus* in the center of *Munich* provides a taste of traditional Bavarian cuisine. In the winter, broad oak tables brimming with laughter and vibrant discussion bring this old beer hall to life. A good assortment of beers pairs well with heavy menu items including roast duck, sausages, and pretzels. Warmth emanates from the festive mood, bringing people together to exchange tales and revel in the companionability of the season.

The *Alte Wurstkuchl* in *Regensburg* blends history and elegance for a more upmarket experience. This restaurant, which has a stunning view of the Danube, is well-known for both its outstanding cuisine and historical importance. Savoring house-made sausages with a zesty sauerkraut, guests take in views of the charming Old Town. The atmosphere of the restaurant exudes an ideal fusion of exquisite eating and history, guaranteeing a memorable dining experience.

IF YOU CONTINUE INTO the countryside, *Rothenburg ob der Tauber* is a quaint hamlet that you will find, particularly in the winter. In the local pubs, where rich stews and roasted meats take center stage, guests may savor seasonal delicacies. The rustic attractiveness of the experience is enhanced by the warmth of the wood-burning stoves. Sample the *Rothenburg Schneeballen*, a distinctive pastry consisting of dough that is deep-fried and topped with a variety of ingredients, such as chocolate or powdered sugar. This delicious dessert embodies winter enjoyment to the fullest.

Nighttime culinary experiences come to life as the sun sets and snowflakes start to dance. In *Berlin*, the *Restaurant Reinstoff* elevates eating to an artistic endeavor. This Michelin-starred restaurant, which is well-known for its creative take on German food, creates seasonal tasting menus that amaze and surprise with each meal. The chefs create a really unforgettable dining experience by combining classic tastes and contemporary methods with a dedication to utilizing local foods.

⁂

A SHORT DISTANCE AWAY, the *Kreuzberger Himmel* provides a special taste combination of German and foreign cuisines. All are welcome at the restaurant's cozy, welcoming ambiance, which serves food that reflects the variety of Berlin's culinary scene. Rich stews and substantial soups are among the comforting and flavorful winter favorites. The lively atmosphere is enhanced by the community eating experience, which invites people to socialize and share their passion for cuisine.

⁂

THE *CULINARY INSTITUTE of Berlin* provides cooking workshops that examine both contemporary methods and classic German recipes for individuals who would rather make their own culinary delights. Under the direction of skilled chefs, participants may learn how to prepare foods like red cabbage and potato pancakes. For those who want to bring a little bit of Germany home, these lessons provide an engaging and entertaining way to experience the regional cuisine.

The culinary delights don't stop at the plate, even though restaurants and winter markets stand out as the highlights of the cuisine. Visits to the region's breweries and wineries are also welcome. Renowned for its Riesling wines, the *Mosel Valley* welcomes visitors to sample wines and learn about the area's rich viticultural history. *Weingut Schmitt*, tucked down amid the vines, offers a quaint environment for tasting fine wines matched with cured meats and handmade cheeses. The winemakers' expertise elevates the experience and encourages customers to recognize the subtleties in the wines they savor.

⚭

IN THE MEANWHILE, THE stunning scenery and storied culinary heritage of the *Black Forest* area beckon exploration. Travelers may sample the cheeses and charcuterie from nearby farms and get a personal taste of the tastes of the area. Cozy lodges and guesthouses can be found in the charming town of *Baiersbronn*. These accommodations are ideal for relaxing after a day of enjoying the picturesque trails and local cuisine.

A world of flavors that warms the heart is revealed by Germany's winter cuisine as the frost covers rooftops and sparkling lights adorn the streets. Every marketplace, eatery, and undiscovered treasure showcases the diverse blend of customs and advancements that define this joyous time of year. More than simply memories, visitors take away a taste of Germany's winter wonderland and are motivated to introduce their loved ones to these delectable treats.

The Hearty Comforts of Bavarian Christmas

Winter creates a tapestry of flavor and warmth in the heart of Bavaria, beckoning guests to partake in the hearty comforts that characterize this joyous time of year. Imagine entering a quaint hamlet with holiday lights twinkling against a background of snow-covered roofs, with the aroma of roasted chestnuts filling the air. The Bavarian Christmas experience develops like a novel, replete with wonderful culinary options and snug accommodations that seem like a home away from home.

Held at the Marienplatz, the *Munich Christmas Market* enthralls with its festive appeal. Crowds anxious to explore are drawn to stalls filled with homemade decorations and seasonal goodies. The Glühwein, a spicy mulled drink that warms both hands and hearts, is a specialty here. While sipping this classic beverage, guests may have *Lebkuchen*, a honey-sweet gingerbread decorated with vibrant frosting and available in a range of sizes and forms. Diners may have a delicious Bavarian feast at the much-loved local restaurant *Wienerwald*, which serves robust dishes like *Schweinshaxe* (roasted pig knuckle) with crispy skin and soft flesh, complimented by potato dumplings and sauerkraut.

ONCE OUTSIDE THE CITY, the historic town of *Rothenburg ob der Tauber* enchants. The town's Christmas market, situated against the background of its well-preserved walls and towers, takes tourists back in time. Wander around the charming shops along the cobblestone streets and indulge in the *Rothenburg Schneeballen*, which are deep-fried pastries dusted with powdered sugar or chocolate. This dessert is a must-try for everyone traveling through the area since it perfectly embodies the spirit of holiday excess.

The *Alte Wurstkuchl* in Regensburg provides a window into the region's culinary customs for a genuine Bavarian experience. Located near the famed Stone Bridge, this ancient sausage restaurant offers you freshly prepared sausages that people have adored for years. The lively environment and the wonderful fragrance of grilled sausages make it an ideal stop after visiting the lovely Old Town. When you pair the meal with a beer from the neighborhood brewery, the dining experience transforms into a historical taste festival.

ANOTHER WINTER PARADISE may be found in the town of *Garmisch-Partenkirchen*, which is tucked away in the Alps' foothills. Tourists come here for the delicious food served in the welcoming lodges as well as the breathtaking mountain vistas. Hearty alpine fare such as *Schwarzbierbraten* (dark beer roast) and *Käsespätzle* (cheese noodles) are the main attraction at the family-run restaurant *Zugspitzblick*. Diners may relax and enjoy their dinner while taking in the view of the snow-capped peaks in this cozy, rustic environment with wooden beams and a roaring fireplace.

SCHWANGAU HAS STUNNING views of Neuschwanstein Castle, which is particularly lovely in the winter, for those looking for a festive getaway. Traditional Bavarian cuisine is served in the *Schlossrestaurant* nearby. Dishes highlight regional ingredients and tried-and-true recipes. Savoring delicacies such as *Rehbraten*, which is roasted venison paired with seasonal vegetables, patrons may take in the picturesque scenery outside the window. Delicious food and breathtaking environment come together to make for a memorable dining experience.

NUREMBERG CHRISTKINDLESMARKT is a magical place to visit, and no Bavarian Christmas would be complete without it. This charming market provides a great selection of goods and foods and is well-known for its signature angel figure. Nuremberg bratwurst is cooked to perfection and served with fresh bread and mustard. Locals get together to enjoy it. People congregate to celebrate the festive mood as a result of the lively ambiance and happy conversation that foster a feeling of community. The lively atmosphere of the market creates the ideal setting for family customs, when both young and elderly make memories while enjoying hot Glühwein and baked goods from regional producers. At several hotels and lodges across the area, the warmth of Bavarian hospitality is evident as the days become cooler.

After a day of exploring, the *Schwarzer Adler* in *Innsbruck* offers the ideal getaway with its combination of contemporary comfort and historic charm. Guests may unwind in comfortable Alpine-style accommodations with views of snow-capped peaks. The delicious breakfast that is served at the on-site restaurant makes sure that guests have a good start to the day.

AFTER A DAY OF TOURING, guests may rest in the cozy setting of *Landhaus Gabriele* in the heart of the Bavarian countryside for a more personal experience. The warm hosts provide breakfast of regional delicacies and insights on local customs and dishes. This lodge's stunning setting encourages visitors to explore the area and enjoy the tranquil beauty of the snow-covered countryside. A trip to one of the numerous breweries in the area would round off a gastronomic excursion in Bavaria. Munich's *Paulaner Bräuhaus* offers a comprehensive introduction to Bavarian beer culture. After samples of many beer varieties matched with substantial pretzels, guided tours provide an inside peek at the brewing process. Both residents and visitors will find the vibrant environment and welcoming personnel to be unforgettable.

CULINARY CLASSES AT Munich's *Bavarian cuisine School* provide participants the chance to study the craft of traditional Bavarian cuisine for those looking for a more hands-on experience. Guests may cook traditional dumplings and *Bayerisches Biergulasch* (Bavarian beer goulash) under the direction of experienced chefs. These courses enhance the whole experience by sharing anecdotes about Bavarian culture and customs in addition to teaching culinary basics.

The spirit of Bavarian Christmas comes alive with every dinner and get-together, enveloping guests in a cloud of coziness, taste, and happiness. The Christmas experience becomes fully integrated with the rich customs and delectable food as the air is filled with laughter and seasonal lights glitter. Every place has its own special charm that beckons visitors to make their own memories among the cozy amenities of this charming area.

Regional Delights of the Rhineland

During the holidays, the Rhineland comes alive and is transformed into a charming scene with sparkling lights and lively marketplaces. This area, which is well-known for its charming castles and verdant vineyards, welcomes the winter months with warmth and charm and provides a feast of locally produced delicacies that satisfies the appetites and sentiments of tourists.

The cathedral's colorful Christmas market in *Cologne* attracts visitors from all around. The streets are lined with stalls bursting with locally made treats and homemade decorations, filling the air with a mix of spicy and sweet odors. With their tempting steaming cups and mouthwatering gingerbread cookies with elaborate frosting, mulled wine stalls are the ideal cure for the winter's cold. Being close to the magnificent Cologne Cathedral makes the experience even better since the gorgeous Gothic building provides a beautiful background for holiday celebrations. Traditional Rhineland fare, such as crispy pig knuckle accompanied with sauerkraut and dumplings, is provided in the *Haxenhaus* restaurant nearby, where patrons may savor authentic regional tastes.

LOCALS CONGREGATE TO the market, which transforms into a glittering paradise when the sun sets, to enjoy the season. Children gesture enthusiastically at the assortment of toys and sweets while laughing and cheery tunes blend together. While perusing the market and taking in the joyful atmosphere and culinary delights like *Reibekuchen*, which are crispy potato pancakes topped with apple sauce and a cherished winter comfort, one may easily lose track of time.

A little distance down the river is the historically and culturally rich city of *Bonn*. Here, the Christmas market spreads out across many squares, each offering handcrafted goods and delectable food. People walking by are enticed to indulge in this seasonal delicacy by the scent of freshly roasted chestnuts filling the air. The historic setting of *Peters Brauhaus* offers a genuine dining experience, while robust German meal is matched with locally made beer. With a rich history, this lively restaurant serves you specialties like *Sauerbraten*, a pot roast cooked in a zesty sauce and topped with potato dumplings and red cabbage.

⟲⟳

TRAVELING FARTHER DOWN the Rhine, the charming village of *Rüdesheim* entices with its enchanted wintertime ambience. In winter, the famed *Drosselgasse*, a winding lane packed with wine bars, becomes a hive of festive activity. In order to beat the winter cold, visitors may enjoy the region's famous *Rüdesheimer Kaffee*, a delectable coffee beverage mixed with brandy and whipped cream and served warm. For those who like music, the *Siegfried's Mechanisches Musikkabinett* is a unique museum with mechanical musical instruments that gives a lovely escape from the busy markets and a window into the past.

Traveling on, *Koblenz*, a stronghold high above the Rhine, offers its own Christmas charm at the *Festung Ehrenbreitstein*. This ancient landmark offers breathtaking views of the river and the surroundings, making it the ideal setting for a joyous excursion. Seasonal activities are held in the stronghold, such as Christmas markets featuring the works of local craftsmen. Strolling around the booths, visitors may discover one-of-a-kind souvenirs and indulge in seasonal cuisine. Warm bowls of *Linseneintopf*, a hearty lentil stew, are a popular option for those who want to eat while visiting the frigid grounds.

⟲⟳

MAINZ'S LIT STREETS come alive with Christmas joy as night falls. Surrounded by gorgeously lighted half-timbered homes, the ancient plaza is overrun with a Christmas market. Local sellers provide a variety of treats that offer a true sense of the season, such as spiced wine and *Stollen*, a typical German fruitcake. The *Mainzer Weinhaus* welcomes visitors to savor the outstanding wines of the area while pairing them with regional specialties to create a gastronomic voyage into the heart of the Rhineland.

THE CHARMING AND COMFORTABLE *Schwarzes Kreuz* hotel in Mainz is a great place to stay if you want to get into the holiday mood. Thanks to its handy location, visitors can quickly visit neighboring markets and tourist destinations while still enjoying friendly service and a substantial breakfast that includes local delicacies.

The charming ambiance of the hotel provides the perfect place to unwind after a day of taking in the vibrant sights and sounds of the city.

Down the river, the peaceful village of *Bad Honnef* offers respite. It is tucked away next to the Siebengebirge mountain range and provides tranquil Rhine walking routes together with stunning vistas. Here, the little cafés offer seasonal fare such as hot chocolate with whipped cream on top and a piece of *Bienenstich*, a delicious cake made from bee stings that is packed with nuts and cream. After a brisk winter trek, this is a lovely place to unwind and take in the stunning scenery while savoring regional specialties.

THE JOYOUS MOOD PERMEATES not only the marketplaces and dining establishments but also the hearts of the people who live in the Rhineland. Friendly locals make the experience even better by extending an invitation to tourists to participate in the festivities. Whether it's the sound of glasses clinking as friends get together to celebrate the season or the joy of kids playing in the snow, every turn brings something new and delightful.

Every stop along the Rhineland route provides a unique mosaic of views, sounds, and sensations that perfectly capture the spirit of German wintertime. This area offers an attractive ambiance where traditions come alive and gastronomic pleasures await at every turn, with vibrant markets, comfortable hotels, and snug restaurants. The comfortable embrace of the Rhineland's winter marvels envelops travelers as they indulge in substantial meals, drink spiced wine, and explore quaint villages, making memories that endure far beyond the final Stollen bite.

CHAPTER 5

WINTER SPORTS AND FROZEN ADVENTURES

WHEN SNOW COVERS GERMANY in the winter, the nation becomes a playground for thrill-seekers and intrepid travelers. There are plenty of options for those hankering for the adrenaline of winter sports, from ice skating on shimmering lakes to skiing down hills. Tucked up in the breathtaking Bavarian Alps, places like *Garmisch-Partenkirchen* became the top winter travel destinations.

Germany's tallest mountain, the famous *Zugspitze*, is located in *Garmisch-Partenkirchen*. This is where the experience goes beyond just skiing, into the heart of the Alps. Visitors are whisked up in a state-of-the-art cable car that offers stunning panoramic views of cold valleys below and snow-capped mountains above. Adventurers may ski on groomed slopes appropriate for all ability levels at the peak. Wide routes for families may be found in the *Zugspitzplatt* region, while experienced skiers seeking a rush from the tough descents can be found there. Warmth and comfort are in store at *Berggasthof Zugspitze*, a quaint mountain lodge that serves substantial Bavarian gastronomy, like creamy goulash and potato dumplings, ideal for replenishing after a day on the slopes.

THE APRÈS-SKI SCENE comes alive as the sun sets, humming with activity. Near the foot of the hills, the *Hochalm* restaurant becomes a bustling meeting place where people congregate around crackling fires, mulled wine, and traditional pretzels. Both residents and visitors have a community experience as a result of the welcoming ambiance, which promotes laughing and tales of the day's exploits.

The charming village of *Mittenwald* is just a short distance away and entices with its breathtaking scenery and lively winter culture. Well-known for its ski schools, this place is perfect for novices who can't wait to hit the slopes. Skiing may be introduced safely and enjoyably thanks to the individualized instruction provided by local experts. For those who are unfamiliar with the activity, the *Kranzberg* location offers moderate slopes. Following an educational day, *Gasthof Post* offers a comfortable haven where visitors can savor delectable regional fare like venison stew and take in the quaint ambiance.

⁓❦⁓

PROCEEDING ON, THE *Allgäu* area provides a further aspect of wintertime enjoyment. *Füssen* is a starting point for adventures, renowned for its fairy-tale castles. Skiing and snowboarding are available on the neighboring *Tegelberg* mountain, which also provides stunning views of the imposing *Neuschwanstein Castle*. The breathtaking scenery is enhanced by the thrilling feeling of sliding down the slopes and capturing views of this famous castle. After a strenuous day on the mountain, *Alpenstuben* greets guests with a typical alpine meal that includes fondue, which warms the spirit. *Füssen* has cross-country skiing routes that wind through picturesque woods and undulating slopes in addition to its ski area. The picturesque paths meander across the *Forggensee* region, offering peaceful exploring possibilities. The fresh winter air is invigorating and lends itself to an easy immersion in the peace and quiet of the natural world. After exploring the icy landscapes, the *Gasthof zum Riesen* nearby is a great place to pause for a hot chocolate or a warm dinner.

⁓❦⁓

THE QUAINT VILLAGE of *Rothenburg ob der Tauber* has a magical ice skating rink in the winter for those who would rather slide on ice than snow. Enclosed by mediaeval ramparts, the rink transforms into an enchanted meeting spot for loved ones. The air is filled with the joyous sounds of music and laughter as skaters gracefully move across the ice. Around the corner, *Café Diller* welcomes guests to unwind with a slice of authentic *Schneeballen*, a fried pastry rolled in powdered sugar that goes great with a hot cup of coffee.

A winter wonderland, *Freiburg* shines in the heart of the Black Forest. It welcomes those who want to participate in winter sports and is well-known for its picturesque slopes and outdoor pursuits. There are several slopes and paths for skiing, snowboarding, and sledding at the *Freiburg Ski Resort*. Guests may unwind in the *Schwarzwaldhaus*, a quaint lodge that offers regional delicacies like black forest cake and substantial sausages, after an exciting day of skiing. With wood decorations and a fireplace that invites guests to settle back and relax, the atmosphere is cozy.

∽✲∾

A BIT FARTHER OUT, snowshoeing enthusiasts may discover undiscovered paths encircled by tall trees covered with snow in the *Schwarzwald* area. Narratives about the forest's past enhance the experience by offering insights into the local flora and wildlife. For tired travelers, the *Gasthof zur Waldschenke* offers a rustic dining experience with filling dishes prepared using ingredients that are found locally.

The exciting sledding slopes at *Alpenpark Neuss* provide a fun-filled family outing where kids and adults can race down the hills while shrieking with joy. The park is a winter delight for all ages, complete with ice skating rink and winter hiking paths. At the *Alpenpark* café, families congregate often to enjoy pastries and hot chocolate while relishing in the happiness that comes from shared experiences.

∽✲∾

NOT TO BE MISSED, *Baden-Baden* welcomes guests to relax following an exciting day of exploration. The town, well-known for its thermal springs, provides a distinctive means of rest and renewal. With its gorgeous snow-covered mountain backdrop and thermal pools and saunas, the *Caracalla Spa* offers an opulent haven. After bathing in the sun, visitors may enjoy a dinner at *Restaurant Le Jardin de France*, which boasts outstanding French cuisine and an extensive wine selection.

AS THE WINTER SEASON unfolds, Germany's enchanting landscapes come alive with excitement and adventure. From exciting skiing to comfortable dining experiences, each place provides a unique approach to appreciate the winter months. Whether it's sliding over ice, skiing down hills, or enjoying delectable winter fare, the allure of winter activities and frozen experiences forges lifelong memories in this stunning nation. More than simply trinkets, travelers take back with them the warmth of fellowship, delectable meals, and beautiful views of the winter scenery, all of which remain carved in their memories for eternity.

Bavarian Alps: Sledding and Skiing

With their expansive slopes and snow-capped summits, the Bavarian Alps captivate tourists as they change into a winter paradise. For those who like skiing and sledding, this area provides a playground where there's always something new to discover and laugh at.

Start your adventure in the charming and bustling town of *Garmisch-Partenkirchen*. Tucked up at the foot of the Alps, it's the ideal starting point for winter adventures. The local tourist office, situated centrally at Bahnhofstraße 24, is a fantastic starting point for information regarding equipment rentals and the finest slopes for your ability level. Skiing, sledding, and dining options are all recommended by the helpful staff, making for a well-rounded trip.

THE *ZUGSPITZE* IS a formidable must-see for skiers. The Zugspitze cable car makes the ascent worthwhile with its breath-taking vistas. The infinite expanse of snow-covered terrain evokes wonder and exhilaration in equal measure. Skiers of all skill levels may find their fit on the more than 20 kilometers of well-maintained slopes here. All year long, the *Gletscherbahnen* (glacier lifts) provide snow for those who want a wintertime thrill. Delicious Bavarian cuisine are served at the *Panorama Restaurant* at the summit, which is a great place to refuel before hitting the slopes.

PARTNACH GORGE IS a great place for sledding aficionados, with an exhilarating toboggan course winding down the mountainside. An amazing ride is created when excitement and the beauty of nature combine. Here, families may explore the gorge and take in the picturesque sledding paths for the whole day.

Just a short stroll from the gorge entrance, the *Partnachklamm Hotel* offers friendly hospitality for visitors looking for a comfortable haven.

The surrounding *Mittenwald*, noted for its traditional wooden cottages and violin-making traditions, provides a pleasant option for those searching for less crowded slopes. Families and novices may enjoy the easy runs on the plateau, which is accessible by the *Karwendelbahn* lift.

With its quaint cafés like *Cafe Gilda*, which serve delicious pastries and hot chocolate that warms you from the inside out, the gorgeous hamlet itself beckons investigation.

FOR THOSE WHO ARE LOOKING for a little more, there is the *Alpenwelt Karwendel* ski area. This location, only a short drive from Mittenwald, offers a wide range of slopes and routes suitable for all ability levels. There are plenty of alternatives, from leisurely runs to rapid descents. For those who want to try something new, the *Bergeralm Ski Resort* is also close by and offers a unique experience with its amusement park and snowboarding facilities. Rest and leisure beckons after a day on the slopes. In Garmisch-Partenkirchen, the *Alpenhof Hotel* provides a comfortable and opulent combination. Its spa, which has hot tubs and saunas, is the perfect place to relax. On the other hand, the intimate *Hotel Edelweiss* offers breathtaking mountain views, making it the ideal place to have a glass of mulled wine and share stories of your exciting day.

ENJOYING SOME BAVARIAN food would be a must-do wintertime activity. There are delicious, soul-warming meals served at local establishments. At the base of the mountain, the *Zugspitze Restaurant* serves classic fare including schnitzel and spaetzle. A wonderful eating experience is produced by the welcoming service and the comfortable ambiance. There are snowshoeing routes that meander through picturesque woodlands for people looking for excitement beyond skiing. *Alpine Sports Garmisch* offers guided trips that take you through beautiful scenery and give you a different angle on the winter beauty. Snowshoeing makes quiet connections with nature possible by opening up often unexplored pathways.

MANY LOCAL BUSINESSES provide rentals and guided experiences in addition to these activities, making it simple for guests to get right into the action without any previous planning. Whether you're looking for sleds, skis, or snowshoes, stores like *Intersport* provide everything you need for an enjoyable day. Youngsters and experienced sportsmen alike are certain to discover the appropriate gear thanks to the expertise of their team.

The Bavarian Alps come alive with holiday lights and winter markets as dusk draws in. The quaint villages are home to stands offering locally produced products, warm beverages, and handmade items, luring tourists to explore a mystical ambiance. *Garmisch-Partenkirchen's Weihnachtsmarkt* becomes a seasonal highlight, attracting throngs to partake in regional delicacies and good cheer due to its upbeat atmosphere.

THE THRILL OF SLEDDING and skiing is calling to everyone in the Bavarian Alps. Every minute is filled with adventure and happiness, whether it's on the Zugspitze slopes or in one of the quaint local restaurants. This magical winter wonderland hides a universe of icy pleasures just waiting to be discovered.

Skating on Frozen Lakes

In Germany, winter opens up a mystical world where pleasure and adventure may be painted on frozen lakes. Imagine the scene: sparkling ice extending over calm lakes, laughter filling the crisp air, and the prospect of lifelong memories.

Set off from Munich in about 30 minutes by rail at *Lake Starnberg*. This charming lake enthralls with its breathtaking vistas and cozy ambience. Locals get together to skate on its frozen surface in the winter. Families are seen wrapped up and sliding hand in hand down the lakefront, their joy resonating against the snow-dusted Alps in the background. Skates are waiting for intrepid explorers at *Sport Müller*, situated at Hauptstraße 3, where equipment rental is conveniently available nearby.

CONVENIENTLY LOCATED on the lakeside, *Café am See* serves up warming treats as the sun sets, illuminating the lake in a golden tint. Delicious pastries and hot cocoa are on the menu, the ideal preamble to an evening of skating. Enjoy a piece of handmade Apfelstrudel while sitting outdoors in the crisp winter air. The warm interior makes a lovely contrast to the chilly exterior.

As you continue into Bavaria, *Eibsee*, which is close to Zugspitze, becomes apparent as a hidden treasure. Skaters and tourists alike are drawn to the spectacular vistas of this gorgeous alpine lake. In the winter, the lake solidifies into a huge ice rink that is surrounded by the majestic Zugspitze. Local stores like *Eibsee Sports*, which is conveniently situated at Eibsee 1, hire out skates to visitors. With its warm fireplace and authentic Bavarian fare, the *Eibsee Hotel* offers a comfortable haven after a day on the ice. After a cold day outdoors, treat yourself to robust foods like Schweinshaxe or Weisswurst.

❦

BERLIN'S *MÜGGELSEE* enthralls with its mix of urban charm and natural beauty, offering a really unique experience. This large lake, which is accessible by public transportation, welcomes visitors and city people to enjoy a winter getaway. Here, skating provides a cool diversion from the busy daily life. In order to keep skaters warm, merchants set up shop along the lakeside promenade, offering beverages and food.

The *Müggelsee Restaurant* is close by and offers a substantial menu that includes hearty soups and traditional German dishes. A cup of goulash soup is the perfect way to wind down after a day of laughing and ice skating as it warms the body and the spirit. If you'd like to stay longer, the *Hotel Müggelturm*, which is close by, has lovely views of the lake and pleasant rooms.

❦

SCHLUCHSEE BECOMES yet another wonderful place as you go north. This beautiful lake in the Black Forest area freezes over and invites skaters to explore its enormous extent. The surrounding snow-covered woods and the crystal-clear waters of the lake form an enchanted scene. Skates may be rented from nearby stores, making it simple for guests to partake in the excitement. Once you've skated, the *Hotel Schiff* nearby provides a comfortable haven. Flammkuchen and Black Forest cake are among the delectable regional fare served there, all served with a touch of authentic Black Forest charm. It's the ideal place to unwind and think back on the events of the day because of the cozy ambiance.

Proceeding along, the *Dümmer See* close to Bremen is notable for its large skating rink. Skaters looking for a quiet place to glide might have a peaceful experience on this less populated lake. The vibrant mood is further enhanced by the regular activities and ice hockey games that the local community hosts. Locals exchange facts about conditions and activities on the official Dümmer See website, which is generally where information about events can be obtained.

❦

THE *DÜMMER RESTAURANT* nearby serves substantial meals with regional tastes when hunger hits. Savor a tasty meal of grilled fish or a cup of hearty potato soup while admiring the breathtaking views of the lake from the eating area. The neighborhood welcomes guests to wander along the coast and take in the quiet of the evening after supper.

If you're itching for a taste of the old world, go to *Lake Constance* in the winter. This lake, which is well-known for its lovely scenery and quaint villages, often has outdoor ice skating rinks erected up along the shore. Festive atmospheres in cities like *Friedrichshafen* and *Konstanz* entice people to spend an evening skating under sparkling lights. After a long day of enjoying winter activities, guests may relax in style at the *Seehotel Friedrichshafen*.

<hr />

DELICIOUS REGIONAL food is served to guests in neighborhood eateries like Friedrichshafen's *SchwabenQuellen*, guaranteeing a genuine experience. Savor delectable cuisine and wines from the area while chatting about your adventures skating on the ice lake.

Many lakeside towns have charming winter markets when the sun sets and the temperature drops, beckoning people to peruse handmade wares while drinking warm Glühwein. These markets often appear around lakes such as *Ammersee* and *Tegernsee*, where ice skating turns into a highlight of the celebration. Everything from unusual presents to seasonal sweets is available to visitors, adding to the lively ambiance.

<hr />

WINTER IN GERMANY IS filled with fun and adventure, whether you're gliding over ice lakes, enjoying substantial Bavarian meals, or cuddling up by a crackling fire.

Every venue welcomes guests to enjoy the beauty of ice skating in stunning environments where joy permeates the atmosphere and lasting memories are created. Lakes become hive minds during this season, with every twist and turn on the ice offering a tale worth sharing. Germany's charms are found in every corner, making winter a time of exploration, coziness, and thrilling enjoyment.

CHAPTER 6
ENCHANTING WINTER VILLAGES

GERMANY'S WINTER TOWNS have an allure that captivates the heart and awakens the senses. These charming villages, tucked away amid snow-capped mountains and sparkling lights, welcome guests with a hearty dose of customs, delectable cuisine, and captivating adventures.

Start your adventure at the historic gem that is *Rothenburg ob der Tauber*, which gleams in the snow. Known as the "Christmas Capital of Germany," this town entices you to stroll along its cobblestone lanes, where it seems as if time has stopped. Festive handmade decorations, mulled wine, and roasted chestnuts line the town square during the *Reiterlesmarkt* Christmas market. In quaint kiosks, local craftspeople showcase their creations, enticing tourists to discover the ideal souvenir of their journey.

THE *HOTEL EISENHUT* is a notable option for overnight guests due to its opulent luxury and historical charm. The hotel, which is housed in a 16th-century structure, provides comfortable rooms with contemporary conveniences and antique decor. A leisurely breakfast that includes regional specialties powers your explorations throughout the day.

The charming town of *Merry Christmas* (Weihnachtsdorf), in *Nürnberg*, is only a short drive away and welcomes visitors with open arms. This lively community, well-known for its Christmas market, is bursting at the seams with vendors selling customary presents and festive food. The renowned Nürnberger Lebkuchen, a spiced gingerbread cookie that has grown to be a Christmas favorite, are not to be missed. The aroma of roasted almonds and cinnamon fills the air as you stroll through the market, transporting you to a sensory paradise.

❦

CONVENIENTLY SITUATED near the market, *Hotel Victoria* is the perfect place to unwind after a day of shopping. It offers the ideal escape from the cold thanks to its cozy atmosphere and welcoming personnel.

Savor a meal of regional favorites, such as Nürnberger Bratwürste, and share stories about your day's experiences.

Proceeding forward, you will come to *Garmisch-Partenkirchen*, a quaint hamlet situated under the Bavarian Alps. This location, which is well-known for its breathtaking scenery and winter activities, draws both thrill-seekers and those who just want to take in the splendor. The hamlet is made more charming by the classic Bavarian architecture, particularly when it is lit up for the holidays.

❦

VISIT THE *KRAFTWERK Garmisch* for a true Bavarian experience, complete with substantial meals and locally brewed beverages. Taste the delicacies of the area with foods like Weisswurst and Pretzel, and enjoy the friendly welcome. After dinner, the *Alpenhof Hotel* nearby provides cozy accommodations with wonderful mountain views. After an exhausting day on the slopes, guests are invited to unwind in the spa. Visit *Mittenwald*, a community known for its violin-making heritage, while the snow gently falls outside. Here the streets resound with music and laughing, and wooden chalets rise tall, coated with snow. A highlight is the *Mittenwalder Weihnachtsmarkt*, which offers delectable sweets and handcrafted goods from the area. Enjoy a nice cup of cocoa or a steaming bowl of *Grießnockerlsuppe*, a hearty soup made with semolina dumplings, while perusing the market.

The *Posthotel Mittenwald*'s quaint furnishings and kind welcome provide for a comfortable stay. After seeing the town, the spa area with its saunas and relaxation rooms encourages you to unwind.

❦

The Magic of Gengenbach's Advent Calendar House

As winter approaches, Gengenbach, tucked away in the center of the Black Forest, unveils its quaint streets decked up with festive décor and sparkling lights. The Advent Calendar House, the focal point of this charming town, is transformed into a seasonal spectacular every December. This majestic building, which was formerly the town hall, catches the essence of the season and draws tourists from all around.

Each year, Gengenbach's Advent Calendar House unveils a new magical scene for every day leading up to Christmas. With 24 beautifully painted windows that light up each evening, the excitement builds as locals and tourists gather in the town square. This stunning tradition attracts thousands who come to witness the spectacle, each window revealing a unique design, complete with colorful characters and intricate details. As the countdown to Christmas progresses, the anticipation grows, turning each evening into a celebration of art and community.

Families and friends congregate to view the artwork, and a festive vibe permeates the air. Gengenbach's allure is not limited to the Advent Calendar House. There are charming cafes and shops on the nearby streets. Don't miss *Café im Alten Rathaus*, where the scent of freshly baked pastries fills the air. Indulge in a warm pretzel or a piece of Black Forest cake here while enjoying scented coffee. The warm atmosphere of the café makes the ideal setting for a respite in between window unveilings.

WALKING AROUND THE village reveals the proud medieval architecture, with streets lined with half-timbered houses that each tell a unique tale. The *Gengenbach Museum*, which is close by and showcases the history and culture of the area, welcomes visitors. The museum, which is situated in a historic structure, has historical displays that highlight regional customs and handicrafts.

For those looking for a more hands-on experience, the local craftsmen provide an opportunity to watch their work in action. Visiting *Weber's Glashütte* gives visitors the chance to witness the glassblowing process in action.

The exquisite hand-blown ornaments produced by this family-run glass factory are ideal as holiday presents. Observing adept craftspeople mold molten glass into exquisite objects offers a unique window into this age-old technique.

THE *HOTEL KLOSTER Gengenbach* is a calm haven after a day of sightseeing. This hotel, which was formerly a monastery, blends old world elegance with contemporary conveniences. Elegantly designed rooms with all the conveniences needed for a comfortable stay allow guests to unwind. The hotel's restaurant, with its warm and pleasant setting, provides regional dishes cooked with fresh, local ingredients. Diners may sample fresh delicacies while staring out over the breathtaking surroundings of the Black Forest. As twilight sets, Gengenbach definitely comes alive. The fragrance of roasted chestnuts wafts through the air, tempting tourists to experience these seasonal pleasures from local merchants. The Christmas market, set up in the town square, has vendors packed with handmade goods, warm drinks, and traditional delicacies. Local craftsmen showcase their products, providing anything from wooden toys to exquisite decorations. Visitors may peruse these unusual products, discovering one-of-a-kind treasures to take home.

While at Gengenbach, consider taking a short stroll to *Klausenstein*, a neighboring overlook that affords panoramic panoramas of the surrounding landscape. This site is particularly lovely during the winter months, when the environment changes into a white paradise. The fresh air invigorates, making it a great site for a tranquil time away from the celebrations.

FOR THOSE INTERESTED in a touch of history, a visit to the *St. Mark's Church* is a must. This remarkable edifice, with its prominent tower and exquisite stained glass windows, contributes to the village's appeal. The church holds special Christmas services over the season, enabling visitors to experience the local customs up close. As the clock strikes six, suspense increases as the next window of the Advent Calendar House lights up. Children are jumping on their toes and their eyes are open with delight as the gathering grows. The tale reveals itself with each unwrapping, creating a joyful and exciting tapestry that captures the essence of the festive season.

⟨◦⧝⧝◦⟩

IN ADDITION TO THE charm of the Advent Calendar, Gengenbach provides a wide range of wintertime pursuits for people of all ages. Ski resorts like *Hornisgrinde* and *Feldberg* nearby draw fans of winter sports. There are plenty of options for sledding, snowboarding, and skiing, with well-kept tracks suitable for all ability levels. Cozy lodges provide warmth and comfort after a thrilling day on the slopes, along with tasty meals that fuel your activities. Snowshoeing along the gorgeous paths is a peaceful way to enjoy the winter scenery for those who prefer a slower pace. The quiet surroundings and the sound of crunching snow make for a relaxing experience. For visitors wishing to explore the stunning Black Forest's hidden treasures, local guides are on hand.

Gengenbach town lights glitter like stars against the night sky, transforming evenings into fantastical stories. Every occasion is infused with the warmth of the community, with laughing and glass clinking filling the air.

Deeply ingrained customs foster relationships between residents and guests alike as they get together to exchange tales and firsthand knowledge.

⟨◦⧝⧝◦⟩

CHRISTMAS IS GETTING closer, and Gengenbach's enchantment never goes away. As a reminder of the pleasure and spirit of the season, each window of the Advent Calendar tells a narrative. This hamlet embodies the spirit of community, history, and culture in a manner that makes a lasting impression, even after the holidays have come and gone. Gengenbach provides an experience that stays in the heart, whether enjoying the festive ambiance, discovering local artisans, or indulging in seasonal sweets.

Oberammergau's Winter Woodcarving Tradition

I n the winter, Oberammergau, in the heart of the Bavarian Alps, comes to life, engulfing guests in a world of rich heritage and artistic creativity. This lovely hamlet, known for its tradition of woodcarving, enthralls with its scenes coated in snow and quaint buildings. The sound of chiseling and carving fills the air as the frost sets in, beckoning visitors and residents alike to see a historically significant art. The winter woodcarving heritage of Oberammergau is still alive and well in the several studios dotting the hamlet. Every store has a cozy, welcoming atmosphere where craftspeople turn raw wood into beautiful sculptures and elaborate miniatures. Frequently, guests congregate around the windows, enthralled by the deft hands sculpting customs and tales into each item. For anybody interested in learning more about this fascinating technique, the *Oberammergau Woodcarving Museum*, situated at *Dorfstraße 8*, is a great place to start. With its vast collection, this museum tells the tale of the history of woodcarving in the area and showcases the artists who have shaped its legacy. From modern designs to classic nativity scenes, one may find a variety of styles here that all capture the creative spirit of the town.

KÜNSTLERHAUS, A SHORT walk from the museum, provides an insight into the life of regional artists. Explore current shows with both known and up-and-coming artists. The café inside offers delicious delicacies, such as freshly baked pastries and locally roasted coffee, and the environment is humming with creativity. It offers a comfortable place to relax, mingle with other art lovers, and take in the atmosphere of the arts.

Throughout Oberammergau's enchanted streets, you can't help but notice the quaint wood-carved façades of the buildings. Every home is uniquely decorated with frescoes that portray religious and folkloric themes. The *Lüftlmalerei*, a distinctive kind of fresco painting exclusive to the area, is one notable example. These vibrant murals are often the focus of guided tours, which provide insights into their meaning and the narratives they tell.

Each stop becomes an experience in itself as knowledgeable guides narrate stories of local folklore and history.

❧❧❧

THE COMMUNITY HAS A unique feel to it during the holidays thanks to the winter markets. Usually hosted in the town square, *Oberammergau's Advent Market* is transformed into a wintry paradise. Wooden booths filled with decorations, handcrafted goods, and delectable seasonal food. As bratwurst sizzles on barbecues and tantalizing odors fill the air, gluhwein warms hands. This is where local craftsmen often set up shop, giving customers the opportunity to buy handmade goods directly from the makers. There's an infectious pleasure and laughter because of this feeling of camaraderie.

A few little eateries provide the ideal break when hunger hits. Situated on *Dorfstraße 22*, *Hotel Alte Post* provides authentic Bavarian cuisine in a rustic atmosphere. A variety of regional beers are served with robust fare like Käsespätzle (cheese noodles) and Schweinshaxe (pork knuckle). It's the perfect place to relax after a day of exploring because of its cozy and inviting atmosphere.

Italian specialties with a Bavarian touch are served at *Pizzeria Ristorante Da Gino* for guests looking for a taste of the local flavor. This place, which is well-known for its wood-fired pizzas, serves a variety of tastes and makes sure that everyone is happy. It's a popular with residents and tourists alike because of the friendly personnel and laid-back attitude.

In Oberammergau, lodging options vary from quaint guesthouses to contemporary hotels, each providing a distinctive experience. Situated at *Poststraße 8*, the *Posthotel Oberammergau* offers a blend of classic Bavarian hospitality and modern amenities. In addition to enjoying pleasant accommodations and breath-taking views of the Alps, guests may unwind in spa services. Its restaurant guarantees an unforgettable dining experience with its seasonal dishes that showcase regional products.

❧❧❧

THE COMMUNITY IS TRANSFORMED into an outdoor playground when winter descends upon it. There are great options for skiing and snowboarding at the adjacent *Kreuzjoch*, with slopes that suit all ability levels.

With so many ski rentals available in the area, families can easily and hassle-free hit the slopes. The lodge at the foot of the mountain provides delectable après-ski cuisine, and friends may congregate to exchange tales of their thrilling mountain experiences.

Snowshoeing tracks meander through the nearby woods for a more serene experience. For those who want to discover the natural beauty of the area while learning about the native plants and animals, guided excursions are offered. This experience offers a special bonding experience with nature, with crisp air energizing the soul and fresh powder crunching under boots.

THE HAMLET COMES TO life in the evenings when the streets are illuminated with Christmas lights. The strains of traditional Bavarian music reverberating across the area often lure visitors. Local bands play and invite onlookers to participate in the festivities. With people from all walks of life coming together to enjoy the season, the vibrant environment helps to create a feeling of community.

Oberammergau's charms go beyond its woodcarving and winter sports. The village's dedication to maintaining its customs is evident everywhere. Events held locally, like the Passion Play, attract visitors from all over the globe, proving the community's deeply ingrained cultural relevance. Every year, tourists look forward to shows that tell the tale of Christ's passion, an occasion that has come to symbolize Oberammergau.

ART AND TRADITION COME together in this enchanted winter paradise to create an experience that everyone who visits will never forget. Oberammergau has a wide range of activities that highlight the splendor of the season, whether it's touring workshops, indulging in culinary treats, or hitting the slopes. This little town creates memories that last long after the snow melts since every second spent there leaves a mark on the heart.

SUMMARY

Take a trip through Germany's winter wonderland, where each turn reveals a new piece of festive happiness and undiscovered treasures to discover. Picture yourself wandering through towns covered in snow, all decked up with sparkling lights and the delicious smells of roasted chestnuts filling the air. Discover charming market squares where people are laughing and merrimenting as the background of old buildings echoes.

The Bavarian Alps are a fantastic playground for winter sports aficionados in this magical world. For all skill levels, skiing and snowboarding at world-class resorts like *Garmisch-Partenkirchen* provide exhilarating experiences. Here, the slopes wind through scenic settings, and quaint hotels, like the *Zugspitze Hotel*, provide friendly service and substantial meals to help you recover after an action-packed day. Winter sports enthusiasts will find the hotel to be the perfect getaway, with breathtaking views and easy access to some of the top ski lines in the area.

***

GO DEEPER INTO THE heart of Bavaria to see the lively woodcarving culture of little communities like Oberammergau. The streets are lined with workshops where craftspeople work to create elaborate sculptures out of blocks of wood. The *Oberammergau Woodcarving Museum* provides insights into the long history of this technique, and the village's creative character is reflected in the distinctive works on display in the local galleries. After exploring the area for the day, relax at the *Hotel Alte Post*, which offers authentic Bavarian cuisine in a rural environment, giving you a taste of the cuisine.

THE ENCHANTED AMBIANCE becomes stronger as the sun sets. Every town has a market, with vibrant vendors selling homemade goods and delectable delicacies. *Nuremberg*'s Advent Market is noteworthy because of its Christkindlesmarkt. Aisles of wooden booths filled with decorations, handcrafted goods, and delicious gingerbread cookies are traversed by guests. Everyone is beckoned to gather around the fireplaces for a moment of cosy celebration as the aroma of mulled wine fills the air.

Discover the magnificent lakes of Bavaria, where the ice rink of winter turns the surrounding countryside into a mesmerizing experience. The stunning mountains that around *Lake Tegernsee* provide the ideal environment for ice skating. Locals walk elegantly on the ice, while adjacent cafés warm chilled fingers with pastries and hot cocoa. *Eiscafé Torino* is a local favorite, noted for its tasty food and pleasant environment, making it a must-stop after a day of skating. Discover the alluring appeal of little villages like Rothenburg ob der Tauber while driving through picturesque countryside. Under a layer of snow, this medieval gem shines, its half-timbered homes providing a picture-perfect scene. The *Rothenburg Christmas Market* captivates guests with its joyous atmosphere while providing handcrafted items, distinctive presents, and delectable regional cuisine. Sample the *Schneeball*, a delicious pastry wrapped in powdered sugar that can be found at *Bakery Riemann* among other bakeries.

***

NOT TO BE MISSED IS the unique Advent Calendar House in the fairy-tale town of Gengenbach, which brings the romance of the holidays to life. Every December day, a new window opens to expose eye-catching exhibits that attract large audiences. With its many stores and cafés where guests may enjoy seasonal fare, the hamlet is a hive of holiday activity. Visit the *Kaffeeküche*, a quaint place to unwind and take in the festive atmosphere, which is well-known for its handcrafted pastries and excellent coffee.

***

EXPLORE THE INTERIOR of Germany, where customs are deeply ingrained. Dresden's lavish Christmas markets, including the well-known Striezelmarkt, beckon visitors. This lively market has booths filled to the brim with ornaments, handicrafts, and the much-loved Stollen, a spiced and marzipan-flavored fruitcake. A trip to the *Dresden Frauenkirche* enhances the experience with a touch of history and stunning architecture. With its rebuilt dome serving as a symbol of optimism after World War II, the cathedral is a testimony to resiliency.

The friendliness of the people of Germany is evident as you make your way through these charming communities. Numerous guesthouses and bed & breakfasts provide comfortable lodging that exudes warmth and charm. Enjoy a pleasant stay in Oberammergau at the *Pension Jäger*, which includes a full breakfast to start the day. Warm hosts often provide insider information, adding a personal touch and suggesting off-the-beaten-path things to enhance the trip.

⟨⟨⟩⟩

SAVOR THE GASTRONOMIC delights of Germany during the winter celebrations. There are many alternatives available, ranging from sophisticated eating in Michelin-starred restaurants to substantial meals in rural pubs. In Deidesheim, sample the fine dining at *Restaurant Ketschauer Hof*, which blends local ingredients with creative cooking methods. Every dish has a backstory that entices diners to partake in a memorable culinary journey.

Adventurers can enjoy winter hiking in this enthralling exploration, following paths that wind through breathtaking scenery and fill the air with the crisp aroma of snow and pine. Numerous paths lead to beautiful vantage points with views of tranquil valleys and snow-capped mountains. These hikes are frequently led by local guides who provide fascinating tales about the area and its past, making each walk an unforgettable experience.

⟨⟨⟩⟩

EVERYWHERE THEY LOOK, art enthusiasts will find inspiration as local artists' inventiveness is showcased in galleries and exhibitions. Germany's winter art scene is thriving, attracting tourists and art enthusiasts alike with its modern installations and traditional crafts. Look out for artisan fairs and pop-up exhibitions that showcase the area's rich cultural diversity and artistic talent.

The spirit of the holidays spreads throughout the journey, fostering relationships between visitors and other adventurers. Every market and get-together has a lively festive vibe that invites everyone to share in the joy of the season. Visitors come away from each experience with treasured memories and a greater understanding of the customs and scenic beauty of Germany in the winter.

⧼◈⧽

THE COMMUNITY'S WARMTH shines through in the midst of the winter's chill, providing a memorable experience full of joy, laughter, and discovery. Every feature of this winter wonderland, from the tranquil lakes to the Alps' slopes, tells a tale just waiting to be discovered. Through the skill of woodcarvers or the joyous atmosphere of market stalls, this stunning nation leaves a lasting impression and satisfies one's inner wanderlust.

9 798224 087143